A Handspindle Treasury

20 YEARS OF SPINNING WISDOM
FROM *SPIN-OFF* MAGAZINE

A Handspindle Treasury

20 YEARS OF SPINNING WISDOM
FROM *SPIN-OFF* MAGAZINE

From the Editors of *Spin-Off* Magazine

with an Introduction
by Priscilla Gibson-Roberts

INTERWEAVE PRESS

Spin-Off Editors, Rita Buchanan, Lee Raven, Deborah Robson,
Project editors, Priscilla Gibson-Roberts, Marilyn Murphy
Project assistants, Carol Leonard, Vicki Yost
Book design and production, Dean Howes
Illustrations, Gayle Ford, Susan Strawn-Bailey
Photography, Joe Coca

Interweave Press
201 East Fourth Street
Loveland, Colorado 80537
USA

Printed in the United States by Kendall Printing Company

Library of Congress Cataloging-In-Publication Data

A handspindle treasury : 20 years of spinning Wisdom from Spin-off Magazine / from the
editors of Spin-off Magazine with an Introduction by Priscilla Gibson-Roberts.
    p. cm.
  ISBN 1-883010-85-3
   1.Hand spinning. I. Spin-off (Loveland, Colo.)
TT847 .H35 2000
746.1'2—dc21   00-061362

First Printing: IWP: 5M:800:KP

Contents

Introduction

Organizing this material from many authors over a twenty-year time span, has been a delightful—and humbling—experience. Reading each of the articles showed this born-again spindler how much I have to learn, to refine, to make my own. The editing process also taught me that handspindle spinners may be in the minority, but we are a dedicated and vocal lot. And our numbers grow daily. Finally, editing this book has allowed me to see my handspindle work within the greater framework of the spinning community.

Flashback to the late 1960s–early 1970s. I was a full-time mom with an unused B.S. and M.S. in textile technology, living in the boondocks of the arid West where my geologist husband's career had taken the family. Pursuing my passion for textiles at the industrial level was not an option. But I determined that I could shift my pursuit to the hand level. Working in isolation, I shed tears of frustration over my first "handspindle" made from a slab of potato with a pencil shoved through it. (I shall never forgive the originator of that ugly idea!) Next came the homemade clunker—not much improvement, as I recall. So I saved my pennies to move ahead to a wonderful little handcrafted spinning wheel. Life was beautiful. Handspindles were history.

Fast-forward to the late 1980s–early 1990s: With family grown, I was now established in my career as a spinner-knitter, primarily researching and writing about historic knitting. Deep into the study of socks, I discovered a crucial fact about spinning: In many parts of the world, the spinning wheel has *not* replaced the handspindle, and this fact was not limited to third-world countries. The common thread to handspinning, I discovered is the high-whorl handspindle.

I felt I had to pursue this avenue. Even with my first plywood-whorl/dowel-shaft/cup-hook piece of work, I was exhilarated by *this* handspinning experience. I had found myself: I was truly born again.

Meanwhile, in the larger spinning community, a mass readiness for handspindles had been growing. Community flashback: The first *Spin-Off* handspindle article in this book was written in 1980. A total of twelve articles appeared between 1980 and 1995. So far there has been only one book available, a little-appreciated gem entitled *Handspindles* by Bette Hochberg. And while this book was on the shelves of many spinners, you seldom saw a dog-eared, bedraggled copy in a spinner's bag. Now fast-forward. In 1995, *Spin-Off* gambles with an entire issue dedicated to handspindles—and wins! Between 1995 and 2000, the magazine will print twenty-two handspindle articles. And by the end of the century, there are two more handspinning books—Connie Delaney's *Spindle Spinning from Novice to Expert* and my own *High Whorling: A Spinner's Guide to an Old World Craft*. Now spinners are standing in line to attend three-day spindle-spinning workshops. As for the high-quality, handcrafted handspindles—try going to any spinning gathering without being distracted by the vendor's splendid offerings.

Do I believe in this mass readiness? Right on! And we have two stellar leaders to thank for preparing us: Bette Hochberg and Ella Baker. Both Bette and Ella were before their time, but at last they know their efforts were not in vain. I consider each to be my mentor, Belle through her wonderful book and Ella through her personal inspiration. Bette and Ella, now we are ready—and we thank you.

Right now, everybody's lives seem locked on fast-forward, with seeming demands on every spare moment. Instant gratifications put us out of touch with the natural rhythms of life. No longer do our activities change with the seasons; we now dictate the seasons in our climate-controlled homes, offices, and cars. No longer do we work by the sun. No longer do we walk to and from our destinations. And with each labor-saving advancement, demands on our time and attention seem to increase.

Result? Stress. We see it with every age group, every walk of life—stress permeates our culture. For the spinning community, stress often translates into squeezing our spinning into bits and pieces of found time. Many of us do not have blocks of time to devote to spinning, so our wheels tend to gather dust. And when we do sit down to our wheels, we tend to push, trying to produce more, more, more. However—and here's the point of this book, maybe of my born-again life—we *can* pick up a handspindle any time, anywhere. Instead of thinking more, more, more, we just spin. And in doing so, we reconnect with the natural rhythms of life. We do not have great expectations; we simply enjoy the peace of the moment. And, in the process of enjoying spinning in these spare moments, we find that our stock of yarn grows. Ed Franquemont expresses this discovery eloquently in his piece on Andean spinning: "Slower by the hour, faster by the week."

I will close this preface with a bit of advice that jelled as I worked on the book. For those of you wanting to encourage beginners, do demonstrate how simple and crude the handspindle can be. Pull out your pencil and slab of potato. Show off that wooden spoon or twig. But when you put a real tool into the hands of real novices, give them the best spindles and the most carefully prepared fibers available. Give them quality on which to build success. Our demand for excellent handspindles has spawned supply. Now we can spin no matter what.

—Priscilla Gibson-Roberts

about Handspindles

We're running several risks in this issue of *Spin-Off* [Spring 1995]. But we're so excited that we've decided to go ahead. The first risk is how much material in this issue is about handspindles. We usually make a very strong effort to balance topics and offer a lot of diversity. But some of the most exciting spinning today is coming from these often-overlooked tools, and we'd like to give you a tour of the possibilities, this intention has disrupted our normal plan.

If you come to this issue with preconceptions about spindle-spinning, prepare to have them shifted a bit to the side. For example, *drop spindles are slow and clumsy.* Or, *you can't be a real spinner without a wheel.* I admit to having—at least subconsciously—harbored the same opinions (despite an awareness of centuries of ancient, unsurpassed textiles) until I noticed my friends (some of whom are incredible spinners) having a tremendous amount of fun . . . and until they introduced me to the "new" generation of spindles.

The second risk is that spindle spinning involves subtleties. The flick of a wrist, a snap of a finger. We've done our best to convey these shades of meaning, through words and as many photographs and drawings as we could pack in. Although getting the knowledge off the pages and into your hands may be frustrating at first, *it's worth the effort.* Be gentle but persistent, and, if possible, share the exploration with a friend.

Third, spindles themselves exist as a sort of found art, often made in very small quantities. We can't tell you where to find one that you'll love. However, we can tell you how to look. Good spindles need to be waited for, seized when they appear, treasured. And each spindle you meet—flawed or perfect—will teach you something at little cost in money or effort.

Our discovery of the delight of spindles means that, for the first time, several of us have gathered at work to spin over lunch. No wheels to haul, no reason not to spin. We're getting to know each other a little better. We still use our wheels at home—but a number of us now have a tiny spinning pack to carry along. It makes life nicer.

You may take the information we present here back to your wheel—great! Many of the tips and projects apply to all types of spinning. Awareness of a tiny hand movement used by some spinners may help you see your drafting or fiber-handling techniques in a new way. You may begin a quest for *your* perfect spindle, which will travel everywhere with you and bring more spinning into your busy life (always a good thing). You may simply read and gain a broader perspective. Whichever approach you take, we hope you enjoy the excursion.

Note: You never know when a casual event will change your life. In 1973, a friend came to visit me, carrying a drop spindle and a bit of wool. He had just learned to make yarn. Knowing I would be intrigued, he loaned me the stuff. I soon discovered that practicing over the bed meant I didn't have to bend over so far to pick up the spindle, which in turn made much less noise when dropped on the soft surface.

By our next meeting, my lumpy yarn hung together and I had been transformed into a spinner, although I didn't know what that meant yet. Twelve of us ordered wheel kits, the Tuesday night let's-figure-this-out group started to meet, and the rest is history.

Life's tidal waves sweep people in and out of our lives. But if it weren't for Bill Ehrlich, I wouldn't be sitting here. If you know him or see him, please say thanks.

And watch out—a spindle might drop into your life, and affect everything that follows!

Spring 1995

Chapter One

SPINNING SIMPLICITY

For all spinners interested in using a handspindle, whether novice or experienced, reviewing the basics is always helpful. For the beginner, review provides insight into the myriad choices that lie ahead. For the experienced, it is a reminder that there is much yet to learn. And we do not learn everything the first time around; we only absorb material at the time and place when it becomes meaningful. So let us start at the beginning.

An Ancient Tool Rediscovered

Whir . . . . Have you heard? There's a quiet revolution under way. Whir. . . . It's spreading from coast to coast, as supporters gather at conferences like SOAR, regional events, and local spin-ins to encourage and teach each other. Whir. . . . Suppliers are responding to this development with newly refined products. Whir. . . . What's going on? It's the rediscovery of handspindles! More and more of today's spinners are finding that these ancient tools fit perfectly into modern life.

"Not for me!", you might protest, especially if you struggled with a drop spindle as a beginner and haven't touched one since. Instead of a calm, steady whir, you might associate spindle spinning with noisy outbursts of "whump!" and "darn!"

But think back. Chances are that as a beginner, you were working with a wobbly old clunker of a spindle. You didn't really understand drafting yet, and who knows what condition the wool was in. Worse yet, you might have been coached by a dutiful but unenthusiastic teacher who didn't like spindle-spinning herself, but insisted that her students had to endure a session with the drop spindle before they could graduate to "real" spinning with a wheel. If that was your introduction, it's no wonder that you're skeptical of handspindles.

Many spinners who were skeptical a few years ago have now become converts. What changed their minds? Perhaps it was watching the graceful movements of a fluent spinner who made spindle-spinning look as easy as breathing. It might have been seeing a lovely skein spun on a spindle, or a finished project made from spindle-spun yarn. Maybe it was finding a lightweight, perfectly balanced spin-dle that whirls like a top. Whatever the turning point, once you've gotten accustomed to using a spindle, it's hard to put it down.

No one is suggesting that you give up your wheel. It's hard for a spindle to match the speed and capacity of today's wheels. But spindles are simple, portable, inexpensive, versatile, practical, and efficient tools, and using them is a very satisfying way to make yarn. You can carry a spindle in your purse or backpack and spin off and on throughout the day, whenever you have a few minutes to spare but don't have time or opportunity to go sit at your wheel. Those minutes add up, and the yarn adds up, too.

Now take that spindle that's been decorating your yarn basket (or languishing in the back of a closet) and give spindle-spinning a try. With a little practice, you too may be joining the new spindle generation.

Spindle talk

A *spindle* or *handspindle* is a small tool that is turned by hand and used for twisting fiber. Basically, every spindle has two parts. The shaft is the slender, straight part, usually made from a piece of wood or cane, a simple stick, or a metal rod. The whorl acts like a flywheel to keep the spindle turning. Whorls can take many forms—a thin or thick disk, a spherical or conical bead, a set of crossarms—and can be made of various materials, such as wood, clay, stone, glass, or metal.

Not all spindles are drop spindles. A *drop spindle* is one that is suspended by the yarn; it does its work in mid-air. By contrast, a *supported spindle* doesn't hang from the yarn; it rests on the ground or floor, in a cup or bowl, or on the spinner's hand or leg.

Many American spinners are most familiar with drop spindles that have a disk-shaped whorl near the base of the shaft and a simple

Rita Buchanan

A high-tech variation: the Support™ spindle, which turns on ball bearings within its base.

notch near the top of the shaft, where you catch the yarn with a half-hitch. Winding on the yarn goes faster if there's a *metal hook, carved slot*, or *spiral groove* instead of the simple notch. Compared to these familiar drop spindles, a *high-whorl drop spindle* looks upside down. It has a disk-shaped or hemispherical whorl at the top of the shaft, with a small metal hook in the center. A *Turkish spindle* is a drop spindle with two cross-arms that slide down onto the shaft. As you spin, you wind the yarn into a ball by wrapping around these arms; when the ball gets too large to keep spinning, you remove it intact by simply pulling out the shaft and then the arms.

Supported spindles take various forms. A *bead whorl spindle*, a very ancient type of tool, has a small, bead-like whorl in the center of a thin wood or cane shaft that tapers to a point on both ends. A *takli* has a coin-sized metal whorl near the base of a thin metal shaft that's pointed on the bottom and shaped into a hook on top. A *Navajo spindle* is the largest type of handspindle, with a broad wooden disk located toward the lower end of a tapered wooden shaft that can be as long as your arm. A *Support™ spindle* is a precisely machined tool with a heavy brass whorl and base and a nylon shaft. In addition to these specialized types of support spindles, you can use a regular drop spindle as a supported spindle, simply by letting the bottom of the shaft rotate on some surface as you spin.

Try to be neat as you wind yarn onto a spindle, because that makes it easier to put more yarn on and to wind it off later. A firm, compact cone or mound of yarn wound onto a spindle is traditionally called a cop.

Spring 1995

*Spindles from: **1**, United States; **2**, Africa, with cotton; **3**, United States; **4**, a mummy bundle, with cotton; **5**, Mexico, with maguey (agave) fiber; **6**, Africa, with cotton; **7**, Mexico, with unknown fiber, possibly wool; **8**, Peru, a grandmother's spindle , used as a supported spindle in the Lake Titicaca area and as a drop spindle in other regions; **9**, India, with cotton; **10**, Africa (Ivory Coast); **11**, Mexico (coastal region of Oaxaca), with cotton; **12**, Peru, old spindle sold in government store, with two-ply cotton. The ceramic spinning bowl is from the United States and the gourd bowl is Mexican. Spindles courtesy of Jeannine Glaves.*

Joe Coca

Hooked Stick

Celia Quinn

The hooked stick is a simple, useful spinning implement used early on in the history of spinning, and has been used in parts of Africa, Asia, and South America even in recent times. In its simplest form, it consists of a straight, thin tree branch with a hook at one end. The hook is formed when a smaller branch is broken off from the main stem, leaving a short length intact. A more elaborate hooked stick, made up of a carved wooden shaft with a metal hook in one end, was used into the twentieth century in Scandinavia. Sometimes a whorl was added near the hook for more momentum.

Uses

A simple hooked stick can be made by using a branch, or by bending a hook at one end of a 10"–12" length of coat hanger wire. It is an excellent, inexpensive tool for quickly teaching children or adults the basic principles of spinning. I even like to get intermediate spinners away from the habits they have developed with their wheels, so I have them take a fresh look at basic principles with the hooked stick. Its compact size also enables it to be carried in your purse, so that you can test the spinning characteristics of a sample of fiber before purchasing it.

Spinning

To begin spinning, hook into the edge of the fiber mass, and twist the hooked stick a little bit in one direction (away from you or towards you, but always in the same way). Draft out a few fibers. Twist a little more. Draft again, keeping your eye constantly on the triangular area where yarn and fiber join. Try to keep the same amount of fiber in the triangle at all times. This will produce a consistent yarn diameter. To do this, draft the fibers at the same rate that the twist is being inserted. If the triangle thickens, you are drafting too slowly relative to the twist. If the triangle thins out, you are drafting too quickly relative to the twist.

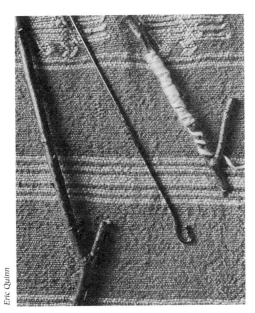

Eric Quinn

Three hooked sticks, the forerunners of supported spindles. A supported spindle was used to spin the cotton for the Mexican huipil in the background.

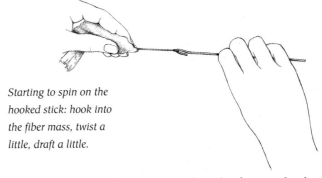

Starting to spin on the hooked stick: hook into the fiber mass, twist a little, draft a little.

Once you have spun a length of yarn, check to see that it has at least the minimum amount of twist required to make a stable yarn. Pull gently on the length of yarn. If it begins to drift apart *at all* as you pull, add extra twist until it stops drifting.

Slide the beginning end of the yarn a few inches down from the hook, and wind it around the shaft by twisting the stick in the same direction as for spinning. Spiral the yarn back up into the hook, being careful to allow for an inch or two of yarn to extend between the hook and the fiber. You're ready for your next length of yarn. Twist a little and draft a little as before, being sure to keep the yarn and hooked stick all in a straight line. If you hold your hooked stick at right angles to the yarn, or even at a lesser angle, the twist doesn't seem to transfer from the hook to the fibers very well, and the yarn wraps around the hook.

Wind the spun yarn around the shaft, spiral the yarn back up into the hook before beginning to spin another length.

Once you get the hang of it and want to go faster, you can roll the hooked stick on your leg. Roll up or down to correspond with the direction in which you were already twisting. Simply roll it down (or up) your leg, pick it up, and roll it again as you spin.

With a little practice, you can pick up a surprising amount of speed on this tool. It is a viable way to produce yarn, as well as a way to share the discovery of spinning with non-spinners of all ages. My friend Elske converted an entire busload of European travelers into hooked stick fanatics. She carved a little hooked stick, gleaned wool from fences, and proceeded to spin while riding on the bus! She has since spun a good-sized bag full of yarn in this way!

So spinners, add a new tool to your collection!

Bibliography

Crowfoot, Grace. *Methods of Hand Spinning in Egypt and the Sudan.* Halifax, England: Bankfield Museum, 1931. Reprinted 1974.

Hochberg, Bette. *Handspindles.* Santa Cruz, California: Bette Hochberg, 1980.

Another hard-working spinner who makes her living entirely from her craft pursuits, Celia Quinn is a spinner, dyer, weaver, knitter, and crocheter. In her fast-paced workshops taught throughout the country, Celia emphasizes fiber properties, control over yarn structure, spinning to a standard, and good planning of the project from start to finish. Besides carrying an intensive teaching load, Celia manages to do plenty of textile experimenting as well as commission spinning.

June 1985

Instructions for a Quick Spindle
Persis Grayson

No class should be deprived of learning to spin because of budget cuts or no money—a good workable spindle can be fashioned from three twigs. Take a 12" long straight stick and lash two smaller 8" sticks (with wool) at right angles to the long stick about 3" from the bottom. It makes a Turkish-type spindle with readily replaceable parts. The most important thing to remember is to make the cross-sticks at least 8" long so that their weight will make the spindle turn easily.

Did you know that you can spin with just a rock? Tightly wind and secure some wool yarn around a fist-sized stone and give it a whirl. Its momentum will allow you to spin a long length, which you can then just wind around the rock. A half hitch will secure the yarn for your next draft. Have fun!

Most of us know Persis Grayson from either taking one of her classes, or from getting to know her through her past column in Shuttle, Spindle and Dyepot. Persis was a mentor at SOAR 1984.

March 1986

Spinning on the Go

Laura Anne Wynholds

Shortly before her departure, Laura completed the project shown above on the loom. She says "it was great to have a piece of handwoven with me." For the warp-faced band, she used a spindle-spun singles from combed Merino top as warp and chocolate-color lamb's wool for the weft.

What do camping trips, train rides, weekend retreats, family reunions, and Interstate 70 all have in common? For a spinner trying to pack, they mean decisions, decisions.

The great question always comes: to take the wheel, or not to take the wheel? For some of us, the problem is which wheel to take or not take. When the travel is via your own yacht, or a giant motor home—hey! You have it made.

But if you're like the rest of us, your travel is more crowded. It involves things like flying, and all that tramping through airports. Or maybe long periods in a small auto with four other faithfuls. Or it's family, so you'll be visiting relations with horrid little goblins who stick suckers in your hair. It's true, sometimes the only answer is to leave the wheel at home.

For the dedicated wheel spinner, leaving the wheel can mean torture, agony, and anxiety. It's like giving up smoking, or chocolate, or you-know-what. A severe and exquisite form of withdrawal.

For the practical, all-purpose spinner it doesn't mean much at all. She or he simply packs a spindle into the trusty carry-on and goes blithely on, happy and perky.

It is logical to take a spindle with you when traveling. Spindles are compact, and easy to protect from the elements and from clumsy people. Spindles range in style and quality as much as or more than spinning wheels do. Great! Let's run down to Bubba Bob's Wool Warehouse and buy a spindle! That way, we'll be ready for the times when a spinning wheel isn't an option. I have a better idea. Let's not, until after we talk about it a little.

Spindles are like friends. When you choose your friends, you do so with taste, with experience and delicacy. You have friends with whom you can speak of great and spectacular things. And you have friends who are only interested in one particular topic. You can confide your innermost self to one friend. Yet to another, you tell only what you want broadcast.

Spindles come in similar variety, and this will affect your choices. It would be peculiar to see someone spinning a cashmere thread on a Navajo spindle. Only a masochist would spin wool rug yarn on a penny spindle. Spindles vary in size, shape, and variety because their purposes and functions cover such dramatically wide territory.

The beginning: the tool

Beginning at the most basic level, there are two major classes of spindles: supported spindles and suspended spindles. (A few spindles fit in both classes, but that's another story.)

Supported means that while working (spinning), part of the spindle (tip or shaft) sits on something—the ground or your leg or a table or a bowl, or something else. The Navajo, the Hopi, and the takli (spindles) are like that. Suspended means that while spinning, the spindle hangs in the air. It dangles from the yarn, entirely or mostly. The Balkan, the Egyptian, the Thai, and the drop (spindles) are like that.

The main difference between the suspended kind and the supported kind has to do with mobility. You can't walk around herding sheep while working with a supported spindle, because part of the spindle has to rest on something. But you can walk around working with a suspended spindle 'til your legs fall off. No problem.

So here is the functional difference between the two types of spindles: one is meant for staying put, and the other one is meant for moving around.

For a spinner who is accustomed to a wheel, being able to kick the seeds out of some pesky kid without having to stop spinning may be a revolutionary idea. But I feel obliged to warn of the effects of drop spindles on cats. Spindles are cat attractants, and it is truly difficult to spin with a cat hitching a ride on your spindle.

Having acquainted ourselves with the two basic types of spindles, we can take a closer look at some practical theory related to spindle spinning.

A spindle is a stick with one or more round things stuck on it. Theory says that any old stick and round thing will work. But if that is so, why do spindles cost so much?

The answer to this question is simple, and it's a matter of balance. This is not a term for the weak of heart. It takes time and care (that means $$$) to make a spindle balanced. Our friend, Theory, says you can use a spoon as a spindle. If you really want to, try it. I don't think you'll become a dedicated spoon-spinner.

A spoon makes a terrible spinning instrument. It does not want to stay upright, and it often spins in three directions instead of two. A balanced spindle spins like the letter I, rotating around its axis. A spoon turns like a X with an attitude.

So a spoon does not rotate easily on any axis useful for yarn spinning. In physics, we're taught that energy can change forms, but it never disappears. As an example, consider what happens when you eat a huge piece of chocolate cake. The energy in the piece of cake—see sugar and fat—is changed into fat and is stored in the body in the appropriate place(s). That is, until you have run around enough to have changed all that energy into work.

When you set an object in motion (for instance, a frying pan aimed at a loved one's head), you are giving the object energy. And that energy can do work—in this case, a concussion, if your aim is good enough. It is the same with a spindle. You put it in motion and it does work. It puts twist into the yarn.

However, when a spindle is not balanced, it uses some of its energy to compensate for the lack of balance. The end result? The spindle does not spin as long as it should, and you have to work your arms off to keep the sucker going.

You are looking for a spindle which spins evenly, for a relative long time, and does not require lots of work to keep it going. As someone who has spun on a well-balanced spindle, I can assure you that you will get a feel for this balance and that it just feels smooth and good. So that is lesson number one. Never waste your money on a spindle which isn't balanced. If you don't have the option of trying the spindle out, you can buy it for looking at, if you want, but don't count on it for spinning.

Now let's look at the spindle anatomy. A spindle has two basic parts, the shaft (the stick part) and one or more whorls (the round-bobble part). The shaft is the axis on which the spindle spins; the whorl(s) provide extra mass, which keeps the spindle spinning longer.

Traditionally, spindles have been made from a combination of materials. I have seen spindles made of metal, wood, glass, ceramic, and stone. Some Roman ones were all glass. Those made from all metal are usually small spindles meant for spinning high-twist (often cotton) yarns. Ceramics and stone show up in whorls.

Spindles made from soft woods (pine, cedar, poplar, and the like) don't seem to last as long as hardwood spindles. Large spindles, the Navajo spindle for instance, are meant for large yarns. Large yarns do not need lots and lots of twist, so you don't need to spin them at high speed and your spindle does not have to be as finely balanced as a tiny spin-

The first step toward a year abroad is packing, "a.k.a. nightmare: everything must be packed, unpacked, and packed again."

Laura denkt bestimmt: Wenn nichts passiert, dann spinne ich eben. *The caption on this photo says, "If nothing's happening, then I'll spin," and it's a play on words. In German, the verb* to spin *has two meanings: to spin (as on a spindle) or to be crazy.*

dle does. Note that I didn't just say, "they don't have to be balanced." It's a matter of degrees. Even large spindles need to be balanced or they will beat you to death.

For those of us who like to spin a middle-sized knitting yarn, a middle-sized hardwood spindle is good. The actual choice of spindle is highly personal. I have a small cherry drop spindle with two whorls (a hook-top Balkan). I enjoy using it to spin a fine, high-twist, knitting yarn, although I could spin just as good a yarn with a range of other spindles.

I am afraid I am not one who cares much about nomenclature. A rose is still a rose by any other name. When buying a spindle, my primary concern is how it spins. The name becomes important if you want a spindle specially made, but normally you can get by with other suitable adjectives. Of course, there are times when a name helps. There are a lot of spindles which fit under the adjectives big or small. But there are not too many that fit the description of hook-top or Turkish or Navajo. Still, there is nothing holy or sacred about the nomenclature.

So now you can consider it safe to go down to Bubba Bob's Wool Warehouse and to buy a spindle.

The middle: technique

Now I am at the place I wanted to start at when I began but couldn't because I needed to build a background. For a spinner changing from a wheel to a spindle, there are noticeable differences. For one thing, you don't have to tromp the treadle. The change in devices leads to a change in technique. For example, you have to keep one hand halfway free to turn the spindle.

Drop spindle technique. That means you can't use one hand just to draw and the other hand just to hold the wool. The hand that holds the wool has to support the spindle, and then it has to stop the twist when the other hand is turning the spindle. This forces yet another difference in technique: the hand holding the wool has to control the drafting zone. This keeps the drafting zone from being filled with twist before it is drawn out. That is okay. You have to do that with a wheel, too.

So what's different? You now have maybe 4 ounces (more than 100 g) of spindle and the law of gravity pulling on the end of your yarn. If you let them, the spindle and yarn will fall toward the ground a lot more quickly than you can put in twist. So you draw out a yarn, with one hand between the wool and the spindle. This hand supports the weight of the spindle and still lets twist get into the fiber-becoming-yarn. If you have never spun on a spindle before, I highly recommend that you do so for a bit, before you read on.

A yarn changes its characteristics with the amount of twist. With too little twist, the yarn just drifts or falls apart. With too much twist, the yarn gets snarly, then weird, and then snaps. But at the beginning, the yarn has no twist and is quite tender until it has enough twist to hold it together.

With a drop spindle, especially the hook-top style, you can put in a lot of twist with a little work (compared to the supported spindle) because there is no friction. You can also roll the spindle between your hand and your leg, not just between your thumb and finger. During the drop-spinning process, one of your hands divides the yarn into two parts. The first part runs between that hand and the spindle. This part of the yarn contains enough twist to carry the weight of the spindle. It also acts as a transfer point which the twist travels through on its way to the second part of the yarn, which is between that hand and the supply of unspun fiber (the second hand).

The hand dividing the yarn has a lot of jobs. It has to draw out the yarn from the fiber by drafting against the wool-holding hand; it has to hold up the weight of the spindle until both parts of the yarn have enough twist; and it has to do all the work of turning the spindle and winding on.

When the spindle needs to be turned, both the upper and lower segments of the yarn need to contain enough twist to support the weight of the spindle. The lower (this is a drop spindle, remember?) hand lets go of its supporting role, the yarn holds the spindle, and the temporarily free hand gets that spindle turning again. The moving-around hand goes up and grasps the yarn close to the upper hand, just under the drafting zone. Then this hand draws out more yarn, and this process continues until the yarn is so long that the spindle hits the floor.

Then you take the spindle in the lower hand and wind on. While this is going on, the upper hand (the one that holds the wool) pinches off the yarn to keep twist from invading the unspun wool. During drafting, of course, the upper hand stops pinching the wool so that it's possible to draft out the fiber. This is the technique for spinning on a drop spindle.

Supported spindle technique. So then comes the supported spindle. This requires a big change of technique for the person who only spins on a flyer wheel, but only a small change for someone accustomed to a great wheel or a charkha.

On a supported spindle, great wheel, or charkha, the actual drafting and pinching off of the twist are done with only one hand. The other hand is occupied with turning the supported spindle, great wheel, or charkha. The spinning process occurs in two stages, which are simple to explain but require practice for success.

Your hand takes the wool in a light grasp, and drafts a yarn with just enough twist to hold it together. Then you pinch the yarn at the drafting zone. Next you hold the yarn under tension while the spindle supplies enough twist for a stable yarn. Then you wind on and spin some more.

The end: travel

Spindles have been in use for thousands of years. They are effective spinning instruments with their own grace and history. I have met a number of people who do not spin on spindles because they felt it was too "hard." It is just different and has to be learned as such. I hope in writing this article to introduce people to the hand spindle, to give them an idea of what they are getting into, and encourage them to investigate spindles and spindle spinning.

Laura Wynholds is unusual among contemporary spinners because she grew up in a family that eats, sleeps, and breathes spinning. One of her early spinning lessons—with Jane Patrick at the Spin·Off Autumn Retreat in 1987—was recorded in a photograph which we printed in "SOAR: The Spin·Off Autumn Retreat, a history" (Winter 1996, page 21).

Summer 1998

Beginning Spinning with Minimal Equipment

Nancy Ellison

A general idea about primitive spinning can be shown with any stick-like object including a wooden spoon. After rolling it along the lap a few times, the excessive twist in the yarn will be enough to twist another length of drawn out wool into yarn.

I teach beginners to spin with inexpensive or make-shift equipment, since many people would hesitate to start if expensive equipment were a prerequisite. Some people only want to spin a small amount, perhaps just make a few projects from their pet dog's hair for sentimental reasons, and those who become addicted to spinning will know what to look for in purchasing spinning wheels and equipment if they wait until they have some experience.

A lot of people who attend a spinning demonstration or class for the first time do not know what spinning really is. To illustrate, I hold up a piece of wool, pull it apart, and ask if a garment could be made from it in this form. I then grasp one end of the piece of wool with one hand and roll it along my lap with the other. The twisted wool has become very strong and cannot easily be pulled apart. Spinning is defined as the twisting of fibers to make a yarn or thread. Lap spinning is actually a very primitive method of spinning with no equipment. (Don't try it while wearing black slacks.)

The preconceived notion is prevalent that spinning wheels are necessary for making yarn. Actually, handspindles do the job just as well, only slower. Accomplished spinners who have always used spinning wheels look down their noses at handspindles as being inferior and primitive, yet for some difficult fibers they are preferred by some people. I know a lady who raises Angora rabbits, who has been spinning Angora on handspindles for over 25 years. Handspindles have other advantages such as being easy to make, taking up little space, and being easily transportable.

I make a handspindle by cutting a round piece of ¾" thick hardwood 3" to 4" in diameter, drilling a ⅜" hole in the middle, and inserting a ⅜" dowel, 12" long, pointed on the bottom end and notched near the top. I always have a quantity of these spindles for students to use or purchase inexpensively.

To begin spinning with a handspindle, one end of a piece of yarn about 2' long is tied to the shaft. Then a half hitch is made at the notch.* The most common method of spinning with a handspindle is to give the spindle a clockwise spin and let it drop suspended in midair from the yarn. The spinner hangs onto the yarn and holds the end against some wool. After the twisting yarn catches into the wool, the wool can be drawn out to the thickness of yarn desired while the spinning spindle twists it into yarn. However, no sooner does the beginner get started than the usual problem begins—the spindle stops going around and may even reverse itself and untwist the yarn, or the wool pulls apart and the spindle drops to the floor. Sometimes I wonder what the people below think when I have a spinning class on the second floor classroom with hardwood floors!

The students keep practicing. Often they have very thick yarn because they have allowed the twist to get into the wool before they have drawn it out. Before long they get the hang of it; their hands are above their heads, and the handspindle has reached the floor. They have made 5' or 6' of yarn and are ready to wind it onto the spindle and repeat the process.

A handspindle technique which I encourage in my classes is for the student to sit on a chair with a book or board on the lap. Rather than dangling the spindle in the air, the bottom point of the spindle rests on the book or board. This way when the spindle quits going around it will just stop rather than start reversing itself. Sometimes there is still enough residual twist in the yarn that wool can continue to be pulled out without setting the spindle in motion immediately. Beginners often overtwist their yarn when they are slow to draw it out. When several feet of yarn have been made with the spindle on the lap, it can then be placed on the floor and more yarn can be spun before winding it up. With the spindle resting on the lap or floor there is less problem with the wool (or more difficult fibers) pulling apart from the weight of the spindle. Instead of sitting on a chair, a person could sit on a rock, bale of hay, park bench, or whatever is handy.

One way to introduce a group of children to spinning is to have them each bring a wooden spoon with a string attached to it. They sit on the floor and roll the handle of the spoon along their laps in the manner of the Navajo spindle technique. Though they probably can't draw out the wool with one hand as they roll the spindle with the other, they can put the spindle (spoon) down and make a length of yarn from the residual twist in their kinky string. Then after giving the spindle a few more rolls along the lap they can make another length of yarn before winding it up. A plain dowel mar be used instead of a wooden spoon, or if they are outdoors they can each find a stick. This is a fun and simple, yet educational way to learn about producing yarn from a mass of fiber.

For many purposes singles yarn is suitable. However, my students learned to ply with the ends of two balls of yarn tied onto the spindle. The singles are twisted together with the spindle going in a counter-clockwise direction. Spinners who have an antique spinning wheel with a small orifice might also consider using a handspindle instead of their wheel when it comes to plying. I happen to enjoy making gadgets, and made a stand to hold two handspindles while plying onto a third. This saves winding the yarn into balls first.

Preparing the wool

For students' first spinning experience I have them use wool in the grease. Depending on the type of fleece, they may be able to spin it directly from the fleece, or just fluff it up or tease it without carding it. I want to make sure they start from scratch and don't get spoiled by using commercially washed and carded wool. They usually find that working with dirty wool isn't so disagreeable after all, and their hands benefit from the lanolin.

I demonstrate washing wool in class by bringing a dishpan of wool that has been soaking in hot water with detergent. The water has cooled to lukewarm by the time I get it to class. I then demonstrate rinsing it in lukewarm water, strongly emphasizing that it is important not to suddenly change the temperature or use too much agitation, or the wool may mat.

Flickering is not mentioned much in this country, as carding has been a more common way to prepare wool for spinning. However, flickering is a way to get by with less equipment. The technique of flickering is to firmly hold a lock of wool in one hand against a board and then brush it with a flicker, which is a small single-hand card. The wool is then released and grasped with the hand around the part that was brushed before. Then the unbrushed end of the lock is brushed, and the wool is ready to spin. Flickering works well with raw wool from breeds of sheep where the wool hangs together in locks.

A flicker is less than half the cost of a pair of cards, but better yet, some items the students may already have may be used instead, such as needlepoint holders for arranging flowers. I once had some dyed-in-the-fleece wool that was matted, and a needlepoint holder helped get it apart, whereas the snarled mats would have bent cards. Some wire dog-grooming brushes are similar to small cards. One brush would be used against a board for flickering or two could

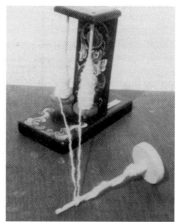

When making 2-ply yarn with handspindles, it saves time to spin on two spindles and then place them in a stand and ply onto the third one instead of using just one spindle and winding onto balls before plying.

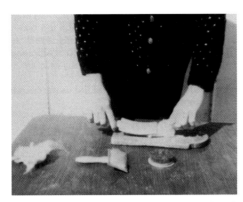

A flicker is a small single card used against a board to brush a lock of wool instead of carding. A dog brush or needlepoint holder for flower arranging are other items that may be used for the purpose.

be used together for carding. My six-year-old daughter likes to card with a pair of dog brushes that are miniature cards just her size.

Some students bring spinning wheels that they've had in the family or have had as an antique decoration standing in their living room. If all the parts are there, usually it is a simple matter to put on a driving band, adjust the tension and start spinning. Most of the old spinning wheels that have come to my classes operate in a similar way to my antique one which is driven by a continuous band that goes around the wheel and bobbin/flyer twice and crosses itself once.

I have retired my fragile antique wheel. I have made other spinning wheels that I bring to class for my students to use and to get ideas for making their own. One is a spindle type that is an easy transition to make after the handspindle because it is like a horizontal handspindle propelled by a foot pedal. I have had a lot of fun spinning on it myself and was as happy as a kid with a new toy the first time I tried it out after constructing it. The yarn doesn't automatically wind on as with a flyer type, but it only takes a few seconds to hold the yarn out to the side to wind it up in a separate procedure. With this type of spinning wheel, students don't need to be worried about the adjustments of a flyer-type spinning wheel. Also, when the wool pulls apart they don't have to thread it through an orifice to get started again.

After the students have spun some yarn, the next question is, "What can we do with it?" They can use regular knitting and cro-

The inexpensive animal combs on the left can do the job of coarsely carding wool. They could also be used to untangle wool before carding on finer cards such as those shown on the right.

cheting patterns for homespun yarn if they make a size of yarn similar to that called for in the directions. I recommend making a sample and measuring it to check their gauge and make changes in the size of needles or hooks accordingly. Keeping a tape measure handy to make sure the item will fit the size of person who will wear it is a good idea. There are also lots of ways to weave over cardboard or wood frames, on backstrap looms, and on many other simple devices.

Usually by the end of the classes (which run from three to eight sessions of two to three hours each and are for adults, but organized through the local schools) the students have gained a great deal of enthusiasm for working with wool. They can come up with some pretty good answers when someone comes along and asks them, "Why don't you just buy your yarn in a store?"

*Ed. Note: on some handspindles, the yarn is tied around the shaft, taken down over the whorl to wrap around a protruding end of the shaft, and then it is half-hitched at the notch.

Here are Nancy Ellison's present-day thoughts:

My philosophy of makeshift equipment has changed to investing in efficient, trouble-free, good-quality equipment and not taking time on anything else. The last time I packed up and moved, I threw my three homemade spinning wheels on the burning pile. One was a walking wheel with a bicycle rim with wooden dowel spokes and spindle; the other two had plywood wheels. One had a bobbin and flyer; the other had a quill. I had decoratively painted all three.

I now have over thirty spinning wheels that include new, used, antiques, and reproductions. Some are part of my permanent collection, other I buy and sell. As I live alone, there is no one to tell me I can't bring home another one.

I seldom organize a series of spinning classes, but I give interested individuals a free introductory lesson and they can try as many wheels as they want to. They usually end up renting or buying one and joining a local spinning group.

Annual 1980

Hand Mechanics for the Handspindle Spinner

Priscilla Gibson-Roberts

Regretfully, I have had a great deal of experience with physical therapists, the result of a genetic defect of the spine. It is amazing, everything we do with our bodies relate directly to the spine. I have also had surgery for carpal tunnel, but have been assured that the damage had nothing to do with the way in which I pursue my dual craft of spinning and knitting. A hand therapist reviewed the hand movements necessary for both handspindle spinning and knitting so that I would be aware of potential dangers, both for myself and, when teaching, for others. I will share these findings so you can evaluate your technique and, if necessary, adapt the way you spin.

Keep in mind that proper hand mechanics are only part of preventing injury. Maintaining excellent whole-body mechanics is critical to support hand mechanics and prevent injuries that can include carpal tunnel syndrome.

Alignment of the hands

Avoid working with your wrists bent. Keeping them even slightly bent, either up or down, can

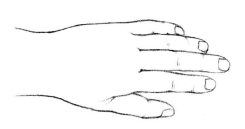

Hand in neutral, at rest position, top view.

cause fatigue and possible wrist damage. When you're spinning, both the drafting hand and the hand controlling the flow of twist should be in a neutral, at rest position. This means that the "V" of the thumb and forefinger should be in a straight line with the middle of the arm, the fingers slightly crooked.

Alignment of the arms

As much as possible, work with your arms in a neutral position to relieve stress at the elbow.

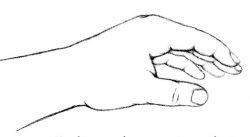

Hand in neutral, at rest position, side view.

Spinning with the fiber supply cradled in the palm of the hand, hand in neutral position. This method works ideally when you use a horizontal draw.

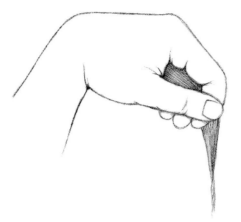

Spinning with the fiber supply cradled in the palm of the hand, hand in stress position. This method happens when you use a vertical draw.

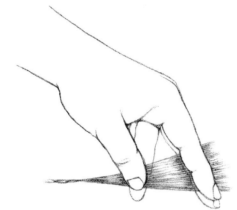

Spinning with the fiber supply between index and second finger, hand in neutral position. This method is ideal for a vertical draw.

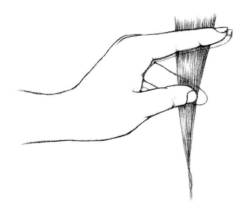

Spinning with the fiber supply between index and second finger, hand in stress position. This often happens when you use a horizontal draw.

When the hands are in neutral position, the wrists should be slightly below elbow level. Spinners using a horizontal draw tend to assume this position naturally. Spinners using a vertical draw should work with their hands one above the other, directly in front of the body with the fiber-supply hand slightly below eye level, the other hand slightly above elbow level. All spinners should wind on with the arms in neutral position.

Aches and pains

Do not self-diagnose a hand, wrist, elbow, shoulder or back problem. If working with the hands and arms in a neutral position does not relieve fatigue or ache, see a medical doctor. Use of over-the-counter supports and braces can lead to loss of muscle strength and exacerbate the condition. Furthermore, there may be a serious underlying condition beyond improper body mechanics that needs attention; use of a self-prescribed support or brace can temporarily mask such a problem. Learning to use the body properly requires commitment; it is a daily, ongoing process for which there is no easy fix. Using a support or brace, unless prescribed and monitored by a physical therapist, is not beneficial.

Priscilla A. Gibson Roberts, no longer traveling and teaching, continues to research and write about high-whorl handspindles and socks. Her book, High Whorling: A Spinner's Guide to an Old World Skill *was published in 1999, and a new sock book,* Simple Socks, Plain & Fancy: A Short-Row Technique for Heel and Toe, *is scheduled for release in late 2000. Meanwhile, Priscilla is once again immersed in recording Eastern ethnic socks, including old world crochet techniques (watch* Spin-Off *for future articles).*

THE SUSPENDED SPINDLE

Most handspinners are familiar with the suspended spindle, commonly referred to as a drop spindle. This is the obligatory spindle for almost all beginning spinners. And for many (especially those who have been spinning for many years), this spindle is usually remembered with considerable distaste. Yes, most of us conquered the rudiments of spinning with a suspended spindle—and moved on to the spinning wheel as soon as possible.

But now it's time to put those old prejudices behind us. Today we have access to beautifully balanced hand-crafted handspindles that make spinning a joy. Even if we use a spindle only as a mobile complement to our stationary spinning wheel, spindles should have a place in the spinner's life.

Why has the suspended spindle been the mainstay of the American novice for so long? In part because it is historically the most common spindle to Western and Northern Europe where traditions carried over to North America with our immigrant population. This was the handspindle that we "knew" about! It is called a suspended or drop spindle because the spindle "hangs" on the newly constructed yarn, suspended on it as more yarn is spun.

There are two types of suspended spindles in this category: the low whorl and the high whorl. To insert twist into the fibers, the former is twirled with the fingers, the latter rolled on the leg. But the two are alike in that, once set in motion, the spinner can use both hands to draft and control the flow of twist in the emerging yarn. Both allow the spinner to move about without interfering with the spinning.

Drop Spindle Basics

Rita Buchanan

Like many spinners, I learned on a drop spindle. In fact, I used it to spin several whole fleeces before I bought my first wheel. Then, like many spinners, I put my spindle away.

Years later, seeing a beautiful skein that someone else had spun on her drop spindle inspired me (challenged me, to be honest) to get mine out again. What a surprise! A fifteen-year rest had done that spindle a lot of good. Instead of the lumpy irregular yarn it used to make, it now spun a lovely smooth yarn.

Of course, the difference was in my hands, but the experience made me reconsider spindle spinning. I started carrying my spindle around, taking it with me when I travel, keeping it on my desk at work, and spinning whenever I have a few minutes to spare. The yarn adds up fast. Here's a quick tally. Since 1990, I've spindle-spun enough yarn for two pairs of socks, two hats, a pair of mittens and a pair of gloves, a woven vest, a knitted vest, a scarf, a little purse, a knitted wash cloth, a woven briefcase, an afghan, and a pillow. All that is yarn that I wouldn't have spun otherwise, even though I still use my wheels a lot.

I'm convinced that a drop spindle is a practical and efficient tool. It's simple, reliable, and versatile, and never needs any adjustment or maintenance. Using a spindle has taught me a lot about drafting and twist, and I've learned how to maintain consistency by eye and by touch, rather than by counting or measuring. But most of all, I spin with a drop spindle because it's enjoyable and satisfying.

A fundamental concept: small, light-weight spindles are best for making thin yarn; big, heavy spindles promote the spinning of thick yarn.

Choosing a drop spindle

It's tempting to choose a drop spindle on the basis of looks alone—colorful wood grain, pretty turnings, and a silky finish have sold many spindles. Prettiness is desirable, but if you're serious about spinning with the spindle, here are four things to check.

1. Check its weight. Does the spindle feel light or heavy? There's a simple relationship here: use light spindles to spin thinner yarns, and heavy spindles to spin thicker yarns. My favorite spindles weigh between 1 and 2 ounces (28–56 g); I use them to spin yarns between 30 and 50 wraps per inch. Some of the spindles on the market today are much heavier than that, but personally, I don't like to use a spindle heavier than 4 ounces (112 g), even for bulky yarns—it's too tiring to hold that much weight at arm's length, and there's no need for it.

2. Is there a shortcut for attaching yarn at the top of the shaft? Some spindles have a spiral groove or a T-shaped notch carved into the wood, so the yarn slips right into place as you wind it up the shaft. Others have a small metal hook screwed into the top of the shaft. Either way, a system like this can speed up your spinning, compared to the alternative of making a half-hitch at the top of the shaft. (If the spindle doesn't have one, you can add a hook yourself. Buy a little brass hook at the hardware store, use a thumbtack to make a starter hole in the center of the shaft, and carefully screw the hook into place. If you don't get the hook perfectly centered at first, you can bend the brass with needle nose pliers to adjust it.)

3. Check to see if the spindle is well balanced. Attach a long leader to the spindle, let the spindle hang down about 2 feet (60 cm), and give it a twirl. It should turn steadily, with no wob-

Rita Buchanan

bling or vibration. If it acts jerky the first time, give it another try, but if you still can't get it to turn steadily, look for another spindle. It's no fun spinning with a wobbly tool.

4. With the spindle suspended from a leader, watch how fast it turns and how long it keeps turning. These vary a lot, depending on what the spindle is made of and how it is shaped, how strongly you twirl it with your fingers, and how thick your yarn is. I like a spindle to keep going a long time, so I don't have to keep reaching down to twirl it, but some spinners just keep one hand near the spindle so they can twirl it as often as needed. You can decide what works for you.

Attaching a leader and getting started

To make Z-twist singles yarn, you need to turn the spindle clockwise. Many spinners have trouble remembering which way to turn the spindle at first, so here's a tip. Stick a piece of masking tape or an adhesive label onto the spindle whorl. Look down on the whorl and position the tape at 12 o'clock, then draw an arrow pointing right. When in doubt, you can refer to the arrow and turn the spindle in that direction (it doesn't matter whether you turn it with your left hand or your right hand).

Get a piece of yarn to use as a leader. Tie one end of it around the shaft, right above the whorl. Now hold the yarn off to one side as you turn the spindle clockwise. Wrap the yarn several times snugly around the shaft near the whorl, then keep turning and let the yarn spiral up the shaft to the top. Catch it in the hook or groove or make a half-hitch and pull it tight.

In England, where I learned to use a drop spindle, it's common to take an extra step and

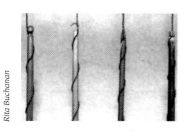

There are a variety of ways to fasten the yarn (or leader) at the top of the shaft: here are a half-hitch that slides into a notch or groove, a metal hook, a spiral groove, and a T-shaped notch.

Rita Buchanan

loop the yarn down around the base of the shaft before bringing it up to the top. What a relief when I learned that you don't have to bother with that! I don't know where the practice originated, but it's a nuisance and quite unnecessary. To review: just turn the spindle clockwise (the same direction that you turn it for spinning), wind the leader up the shaft, making several turns and holding the yarn taut; leaving a tail that's a few inches long, secure the leader to the top of the spindle, and you're ready to spin.

Join the fiber onto the leader as you usually would—overlap by a distance equal to the average fiber length and twist the ends together. When you're doing this, it helps if you support the bottom of the spindle by resting it on your leg or chair. As soon as the join is well twisted, you can let the spindle drop again.

Holding the fiber

I see most spinners holding the fiber in their left hand and turning the spindle with their right hand, but you can try it the other way if you want. Either way, the hand that holds the fiber will be busy. You need to hold the fiber out of the way so it doesn't get caught in the yarn, regulate the flow of fibers into the drafting zone, and pinch off the twist so it doesn't run up into the fiber supply. The pictures show different ways of holding different fiber preparations; try them all to see which is most comfortable for you.

Priscilla Gibson-Roberts

To hold more fiber and make fewer joins, wrap a piece of roving or an attenuated batt around your wrist. Bring the end down between your thumb and index finger, and hold it there.

Spinning

You can spin sitting down or standing up (or walking around!), whichever you prefer. Sitting works fine, even though you can't make a very long piece of yarn before you have to stop and wind on. If you have a handy hook or groove, winding on isn't much of an interruption. We've all heard jokes about standing on a balcony and letting the spindle drop all

Some spinners find it easier to hold a tuft of fiber between their index and second fingers, and to pinch off the twist with their thumb and ring finger or little finger.

To spin from a rolag, try cradling the fiber in the palm of your hand and pinching off the twist with your thumb and index finger. To avoid catching the rolag in the forming yarn, tuck the end under a bracelet, watchband, rubber band, etc.

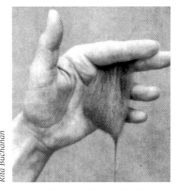

To spin from the fold, try holding the ends of the fibers between your index and second fingers, with the fold pointing down toward the spindle. You can use your thumb and little finger to control the drafting and twist.

the way to the ground, but in fact such a long piece of yarn would probably get completely snarled or untwisted before you could wind it on.

I could go on and on about different ways of holding your hands and drafting, but basically, if you can spin on a wheel now, you'll be able to spin on a drop spindle. Take a fiber you're familiar with and give it a try. You can do short draw, long draw, worsted, woolen, point-of-contact—

whatever you call it and whatever you do, you can do it on a drop spindle, too.

I usually choose my drafting technique on the basis of fiber length. If the fibers are about 3 to 4 inches (7.5 to 10 cm) long or longer, I spin with a short draw: I twirl the spindle, pinch the yarn just below the drafting zone, pull down about one-half the fiber length, and let go. I keep pinching and pulling until I have to reach down and twirl the spindle again, then repeat. If the fibers are shorter than that, I spin with a long draw: I twirl the spindle, then pinch the yarn lightly, so the twist can run right up to the drafting triangle, and keep pulling the yarn down in one slow, continuous gesture. My hands may be 2 or 3 feet (60 to 90 cm) apart by the time I have to reach down and twirl the spindle again.

Either way, short draw or long draw, I like to hold the fiber just above my face. One of my favorite things about spinning is watching the drafting zone, where the fibers pull out of the fiber supply and are twisted into the yarn, and one of the nice things about drop-spindle spinning is that I can position the drafting zone where it's easy to watch. I see other spinners do this, too, and here's what happens. After watching the drafting zone for a while, a spinner's face takes on a certain rapt expression, accompanied by a feeling of calm satisfaction.

You can get that feeling at the wheel, too, but I associate it more with spindle spinning.

To maintain consistency, make a sample by breaking off a length of yarn, tying the two ends together, and letting it double back on itself. Keep that sample handy. As you spin, stop from time to time, let some yarn double back on itself, and compare it with the sample. Feel them both between your thumb and finger—are they the same thickness? Hold them side by side and compare the angle of twist or number of twists per inch—are they the same? Keep referring to the sample and check yourself often. With practice, you can spin a very uniform yarn on a drop spindle.

Winding on and winding off

When it's time to wind on, pinch off the twist with the hand that's holding the fiber and reach

Turn the spindle in the same direction to wind on the yarn as you turn it for spinning, then keep turning as you spiral the yarn up the shaft. You don't have to loop the yarn around the shaft under the whorl, as shown in many spinning books. That's an extra step that just slows you down.

down to catch the spindle with your other hand. Keep your hands apart and hold the yarn under tension so it can't kink into snarls as you wind it on. Layer after layer, build up a solid cone of yarn, nestled snugly against the whorl. Remember to stop winding before you reach the end of the yarn. Leaving a few inches between the top of the spindle and the fiber supply makes it easier to start spinning again.

Being careful to wind on neatly isn't just a fussy habit—it's a lesson learned from experience. You can put a lot more yarn on the spindle, and you'll have fewer tangles getting it off, if you wind firmly and compactly. How much you fill the spindle is up to you. I react to the increased weight, and usually stop before the yarn weighs as much as the spindle itself; that is, I spin less than 1 ounce of yarn onto a 1-ounce spindle.

Sit or stand, whichever you prefer, when using a drop spindle. Either way, the spinning action is right in front of your face, where it's easy to see what you're doing. Many spinners think watching the drafting zone is a lot more fascinating than what's on TV. The spinner here is Jenny Bakriges of Middletown, Connecticut, who carries her drop spindle everywhere and uses it to make beautiful knitting yarns.

Some spinners prefer to use a ball winder, but I like to unwind my singles yarn into a nice round ball. The hardest part of making a ball is getting it started, so I use a felt ball for a core and start winding around that. Unwinding goes fastest if you can recruit a partner to hold the spindle by both ends. Otherwise, you can hold the ball in one hand and the spindle with the other hand—or construct gentle supports to hold the ends of the spindle.

Now here's one of my favorite tricks to use when you're spinning a lot of the same yarn. Wind the first spindleful onto a ball, then spin another spindleful. Take each of the ends—one from the ball and one from the spindle, and untwist them enough to loosen the fibers. Overlap the loosened fibers, like making a join, and twist them together. Ta-da! Continuous yarn! If you keep doing this, one spindle after another, you can make a ball of yarn as big as you like, with no knots or breaks. As a rule of thumb, a ball the size of a small grapefruit is enough to make a hat, a scarf, or a pair of mittens. A ball as big as a cantaloupe or honeydew melon is enough to knit a vest.

Plying

Of course you can ply on a drop spindle. Plying goes faster than spinning, and you don't have to watch it so closely. The one challenge is holding the yarn that you want to ply. I usually set two or three balls in separate mixing bowls on the floor beside me. If I want to ply while I'm going for a walk (this is easier than it sounds), I take the ends of two or three balls, hold them as one, and rewind the yarn into a single ball that I can hold in my hand. If you like using a ball

The easiest way to unwind is to recruit an assistant to hold the ends of the spindle. When you're alone, you can stick the ends through holes punched in a shoebox, or hold the spindle with one hand and the ball or niddy noddy with the other hand.

Plying on a drop spindle is easy. Just unwind some yarn and twist the spindle counterclockwise. Keep an eye on the yarn; when you think it's twisted enough, stop and wind it on.

Catching the yarn behind your elbow is another way to keep it straightened out as you're winding it on. Here Jenny is plying, by using both ends from a center-pull ball. Notice how she puts her thumb through the middle of the ball, to keep the yarn from collapsing into a snarl.

winder and plying from both ends of a center-pull ball, try that.

In any case, unwind an arm's length of yarn from the ball(s), twist the spindle counterclockwise for S twist, and let the twist run up the yarn. If you kept a doubled-back sample of the singles yarn, refer to that now, and twist the plied yarn until it matches the sample. Or just twist until you like the looks of the plied yarn. Then stop and wind on. Remember to turn the spindle in the same direction to wind on the yarn as you do to spin it; for plying, wind on counterclockwise.

I usually use a larger drop spindle for plying than for spinning, so I can wind more yarn onto it. After plying, I usually wind off onto a niddy noddy and make skeins, instead of balls, because I always like to wash my yarn before using it.

If you're spinning a lot of yarn and want to make a continuous ball with no breaks or knots, splice the ends together each time you add more yarn. Take both yarn ends—the one from the spindle and the one from the ball—and loosen the fibers. Overlap the ends and hold them in place as you twist them together, like making any join. Resting the spindle on a table makes this job easier. The ball in the picture already contains about twenty spindlefuls of yarn.

Rita Buchanan keeps most of her spindles and wheels at home in Connecticut, although some of them are very well traveled—especially the spindles.

Spring 1995

The High-whorl Spindle

Priscilla A. Gibson-Roberts

Had anyone indicated, back at the beginning of my spinning career, that I would someday become a handspindle enthusiast, I would have laughed. At the time, I couldn't move on to a spinning wheel fast enough! Now, I realize that it was not only my lack of skills that frustrated me, but also the handspindle itself.

My disdain for the handspindle continued through many years. Then I began to study ethnic socks. I found that in many parts of the world, the spinning wheel never replaced the handspindle. One region where the spindle and the wheel coexisted was the North Sea Islands and Scandinavia. As the scope of my research increased, I found the same to be true in parts of Eastern Europe. And for spinning sock yarns in the Middle East, the handspindle was the tool of choice.

Obviously, these people knew something that I did not. Upon studying the spindles, I found a common thread that connected all these areas: the preferred spindle was most often a hooked, high-whorl spindle. This avenue clearly needed some exploration. My findings were verified by a study of Bette Hochberg's Handspindles (a gem of a book that I hadn't previously appreciated).

The spindle itself

The next step was experimentation. To my surprise, even a poorly crafted homemade version of the high-whorl spindle served quite nicely. But clearly, I am not alone in my pursuit of this tool, for today some beautifully crafted ones are commercially available. I'm not a collector, per se, but I have acquired several high-whorl spindles of my own and tried others at workshops. Based on this experience, I suggest the following guidelines for choosing a high-whorl spindle.

Two of the most important considerations are size and weight. In general, a large spindle works best for medium to heavy yarns (sportweight to worsted weight, in the vernacular of knitters), and a small spindle is best for fine yarns (fingering to lace weight). The large spindle should weigh between 50 and 85 grams (about 2 to 3 ounces), depending on whether you prefer a gentle or

A woman named Ayse spins wool on a high-whorl spindle, Istanbul, 1978.

Photo by Betsy Harrell (author of Anatolian Knitting Designs, Istanbul: Redhouse Press, 1981), used by kind permission. Betsy's note on the slide recalls that "everyone called her 'Deaf Ayse.'"

Some excellent, commercially available, high-whorl spindles (clockwise, bottom to top): large Icelandic birch and Norsk cherry (with threaded whorl) spindle; small Icelandic birch and New Zealand wool spindles.

strong draw (the heavier the spindle, the stronger the draw). The shaft should be about 12 to 15 inches (30 to 37.5 cm) long—enough shaft to allow for yarn storage and rolling the spindle, but not so much that it limits how far the spindle can drop before hitting the floor. The most desirable small spindles weigh 12 to 15 grams (about 1/2 ounce) and have a shaft 7 to 8.5 inches (17.5 to 21 cm) long.

In all cases, the hook should be durable and not easily bent out of shape. Test it with your finger—don't judge by the diameter of the metal, because a hook can be very fine yet incredibly strong. The hook must be positioned at the center

Hand-carved, flower-whorl spindles, created by folk artist Otis Gillespie of Penrose, Colorado. The petals create notches to secure the yarn as it passes up to the hook. The spindle at left has interchangeable whorls of two different weights with square fitting about round shaft. Alas, not for sale. . . .

of gravity, or the spindle will wobble. Attach a length of yarn and twist the spindle to see how it behaves.

Take a look at the whorl. Sometimes there are one or more notches cut into the edge of the whorl, to serve as a catch for the yarn as it passes from the shaft up to the hook. (You can always cut such a notch yourself, using a fine craft knife.) Often the whorl is glued in place, but some top-whorl spindles have a removable whorl, a nice feature that simplifies winding off to skein the yarn. A removable whorl may attach to the shaft by a threaded fitting, a square fitting, or a simple friction fit.

Using the high-whorl spindle

I love the high-whorl spindle for its ease of use and its versatility. No more twirling the shaft with arthritic fingers, because the high-whorl spindle is set into motion by rolling it on the thigh with the palm of the hand. No more frustrating half-hitches to work and unwork before and after each length of yarn, because the yarn is secured on the hook with a turn of the shaft. The rolling action is very efficient—one roll is enough to twist an entire length of yarn. And not only can the spindle be used suspended for worsted-type yarns, but it can also be used supported for softer, woolen-type yarns. Finally, I find that I spend more time spinning these days because the spindle is always at my side. No longer do I have to trot upstairs to the spinning wheel in its fixed location. It's amazing how much yarn can be spun in five-minute intervals throughout the day.

Following is my way for using the high-whorl spindle, not *the* way. Some of my working techniques are quite traditional; others are unorthodox. As I suggest in my workshops, experiment to find out which serve you and which do not.

First, I prepare a leader from about a yard of brightly colored, medium-weight, plied yarn. Bringing the ends together, I tie an overhand knot to make a large loop. With the knotted end at the shaft, I encircle the shaft and draw the end of the loop through at the knot, then follow with a half-hitch to securely fasten the leader.

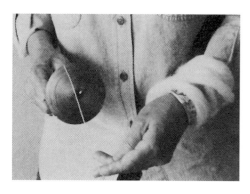

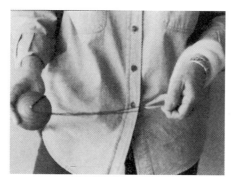

far right: When spinning Z, lay the leader (or spun yarn) to the right of the hook, then turn the spindle clockwise to catch the yarn into the hook.

Right: Lay a wisp of fibers into the loop of the leader, to secure the fiber supply to the spindle.

When spinning Z, lay the leader (or spun yarn) to the right of the hook, turning the spindle clockwise to catch the yarn into the hook. When spinning S, lay the leader (or spun yarn) to the left of the hook and turn counterclockwise to catch the yarn into the hook. Draw out a wisp of prepared fibers, tucking them through the end of the loop, then turn the shaft by hand to secure the fiber to the leader. In Eastern fashion, I use my arm as a distaff, wrapping the prepared fibers around my wrist—or into my sleeve, when wearing a long-sleeved shirt. (This eliminates the frustration of having the fiber supply wrap around the newly spun yarn.)

To start the spinning process, begin to draw out the fibers before rolling the spindle. Twist is inserted so rapidly with this spindle that this initial drafting gives you time to move your hand into position before twist can enter the fiber supply. Then continue to draft as far as you can comfortably reach, and let the twist run along the yarn.

You can hold the fiber supply in either hand, left or right. With fiber in the left hand, Z twist is inserted by rolling the shaft up the right thigh, S twist by rolling down the right thigh. With fiber in the right hand, Z twist is inserted by rolling down the left thigh, S twist by rolling up the left thigh. For many spinners, accustomed to a Saxony-type spinning wheel and holding the fiber supply in the right hand, continuing in this manner is easier. I found this to be true in my case—until this past summer. Then I found the reasoning behind the more traditional method of holding fiber in the left hand and rolling up the right thigh. Most of us are right-handed; therefore, when the fiber supply is to the left, it is easy to hang onto the spindle with the left hand while freeing the right to stir the pot on the fire, catch the grandchild about to take a swim in a fast-moving stream, or

respond to other emergencies. One spinning session while camping put me into the traditional mode in a hurry!

When a length of yarn has been spun, grasp the bottom of the shaft, swinging the whorl away from your body. When spinning Z, a counterclockwise turn releases the yarn from the hook. Then turn the shaft clockwise to wind the yarn onto the shaft. (Reverse for S twist.) I prefer to store the yarn in the somewhat rounded "beehive" shape often seen in the Middle East rather than the classic "cone" often recommended in many spinning books, because I find it makes my style of plying easier.

As I'm spinning, I keep both hands in front of me on a level plane, rather than holding one hand above the other. The newly spun yarn runs over the curved fingers of my right hand and down to the spindle. My right thumb and forefinger control the advancing twist while the left hand draws away to the side. This position has several advantages. For someone who wears trifo

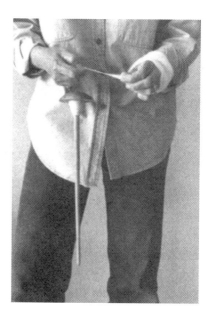

Start drafting out the fibers before you set the spindle into motion. This drafted length will absorb the initial twist, giving the hand that turns the spindle and regulates the twist time to get into position before the twist runs up into the fiber supply.

Right: To wind on a length of yarn, grasp the base of the shaft and swing the spindle away from your body. Turn it counterclockwise to release the yarn from the hook, then turn it clockwise again to wind the yarn onto the shaft.

Above: Spinning is less tiring, and it's easier to see what you're doing, if you hold your two hands on a level plane, rather than one above the other. In this position, the motions are just like drafting at the spinning wheel.

cals like I do, it's easier to bring the yarn into focus and watch what you're doing. With both hands on a level plane, the drafting action is the same as at the spinning wheel. Keeping the fiber supply off to the side helps keep unspun fibers from getting tangled in the yarn. And holding both hands down is not as tiring as holding one hand up high in the air.

You can spin standing up or sitting down. If you're standing up or wearing a skirt, it's easiest to roll the spindle against the outside of your thigh. But if you're sitting down and wearing pants, you can roll the spindle on the inside of

your thigh. This keeps the action centered, so you don't have to twist your body to the side or bring the rotating spindle forward around your legs. I have spent hours spinning in this manner while sitting in airports without attracting undue attention.

Plying

Plying on a handspindle is all too often ignored. There are many ways to ply, some more frustrating than others. For medium- to heavy-weight yarns, I ply from two center-pull "balls." After spinning, I slip the cop of yarn off the shaft directly onto a wooden knitting needle, or a smooth wooden dowel sharpened in a pencil sharpener. The base of the cop, and the bright-colored leader, will be at the pointed end of the needle. I remove the leader and set it aside for future use.

When I have two cops, I hold them in my right hand, lay the two singles into the loop of the leader on the spindle, and roll the shaft up my left thigh to insert S twist. (Or, you could hold the two needles in your left hand and roll the spindle down your right thigh to insert S twist.) The singles feed out from the centers of the cops, and since the centers are secured by the knitting needles, any tangles are easily undone.

For fine yarns, I wind the singles off onto my nøstepinne (a Norwegian yarn-winding stick,

Right: If you're wearing pants, you can spin sitting down by rolling the spindle against the inside of your thigh. This is a comfortable gesture and an unobtrusive way to spin at meetings or in public places. Roll up the inside of your left thigh, as shown here, for Z twist.

Below: If you're holding the fiber with your left hand, roll the spindle up your right thigh for Z twist. Wrapping the fiber around your arm helps keep it from getting snarled in the yarn.

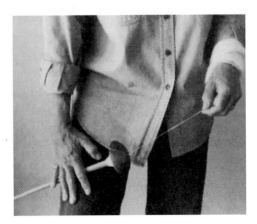

used for making center-pull balls). I then ply from both ends of the ball, leaving the ball on the nøstepinne. I have a favorite nøstepinne reserved for spindle spinning only; it was hand-crafted by Ken Slemko of Canada and has a steep angle between top and bottom and a shallow groove at the top. This allows me to move the ball up to the top, where the yarn is free to move more easily; the shallow groove does not catch the yarn.

Incidentally, it is not wise to check for balanced twist by allowing the yarn to relax and test for ply-back. If the yarn was spun over a period of time, the Z twist has set, making the ply-back test unreliable. To detemine the amount of twist for plying, spin a section of yarn and let it double back on itself immediately, then save this sample and refer to it as you ply.

After plying, I wind off the yarn into skeins for finishing. For winding off, a removable whorl is nice, but not necessary. If I'm standing up, I put the shaft between my ankles with the whorl to the back. This keeps the spindle from wildly bouncing around the area. If sitting, I keep the whorl down in my lap. This works best when wearing a skirt that can cup the whorl, but a lap cloth or apron works for jeans.

Supported-spindle technique

Up to this point, I have described using the spindle for worsted-type yarns—spinning with the tool suspended. This is the preferred method for yarns requiring relatively high twist, such as the sock yarns I typically spin these days. But this type of spindle can also be used in a supported position, to produce a soft, low-twist, woolen-type yarn for sweaters. The process is the same except that the shaft is always resting on the thigh, thus eliminating the need to twist the yarn so much that it is strong enough to bear the weight of the spindle. In supported spinning, one hand rolls the spindle on the thigh while the other hand draws out the fibers against the advancing twist.

Left: To ply thinner yarn, Priscilla first winds it onto a nøstepinne—a tapered wooden peg—to make a center-pull ball, and takes both ends to make a two-ply yarn.

Conclusion

Has my love for this type of spindle replaced my spinning wheel? Not yet, because when I want to produce a large quantity of yarn for a sweater I still prefer the wheel. But now my love for ethnic socks has all but replaced my former desire to knit sweaters. I seem to move forward by stepping back in time!

Above: By supporting it on your thigh, you can use a high-whorl spindle to make a soft, low-twist yarn. One hand rolls the spindle, and the other hand drafts the fiber away from the twist.

Spring 1995

Turkish Spindle

A Turkish spindle has two crossarms that slide onto the shaft. As you spin, you wind the yarn into a ball by wrapping around these arms. When the ball gets too large to keep spinning, you can pull apart the spindle, and the ball remains intact. It's a nifty trick, although winding yarn onto a Turkish spindle goes much more slowly than winding onto a regular spindle. Some Turkish spindles have two sets of crossarms which can be used separately or in combination to vary the spindle's weight.

Spring 1995

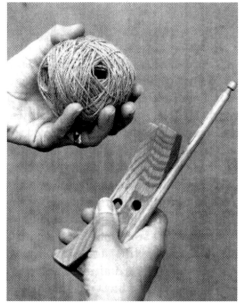

Chapter Three

THE SUPPORTED SPINDLE

Supported spindles come in many shapes and sizes, from the large Salish and Navajo spindles to the small bead spindles of Africa and the takli of India—with a lot of spindles in between those extremes! While used in many ways, all have certain characteristics in common. First, all have some sort of support: they may rest on the ground, on the thigh, in a bowl, or in the hand. Second, all require that only one hand hold and draft the fiber supply while the other hand attends to twisting the yarn by whatever means the specific spindle provides. Third, the spinner cannot depend on counting and measuring to spin a consistent yarn, but must instead hone the eye to see and the hand to feel when the yarn is properly spun. Techniques differ from one type of spindle to the other, but all can be used to spin incomparably wonderful yarns.

In Support of Supported Spindles

Lee Raven

Most of us who do a bit of teaching wonder at times whether we're doing the best job we can. Because we have accepted the responsibility for sharing reliable information, we continue to school ourselves in every component of yarn construction. We strive to become more aware of the functions and limitations of our tools and to become masters of our manual skills. Our clearer understanding of the elements of our craft provides our students with a sturdier foundation from which to base their own explorations.

When I learned to spin my teacher took the very sensible approach of starting me on the drop spindle to learn the basics of yarn construction without the complications of wheel mechanics. Once I was comfortable with the drop spindle, I moved onto the flyer wheel. Later as I began to teach others, I followed the same approach of teaching drop spindle first, flyer wheel second.

But the mastery of spinning doesn't end with the mastery of the flyer and bobbin wheel. On a time scale of Spinning Tools and Technology, the use of flyer and bobbin wheels take up less than one quarter of one percent of the space. It is we who have chosen to identify with that little portion of history and focus upon it as the apex of hand spinning. I would like to suggest that taking a few steps backwards on that scale may well enhance your mastery of the crafts, and even make you a better teacher.

Try taking a closer look at spindle wheels, one step earlier on the scale, and precursors of the flyer and bobbin wheels. Any hand-turned spindle wheel will do: the great wheel, the charkha, or the cord-rimmed wheels of Asia. What are the essential differences in producing a yarn on a spindle wheel instead of a flyer wheel? One is that we tend to think of them as being

slower wheels because wind-on is a separate step. Another is that the tug of the wheel has been eliminated, increasing the range of fine yarn sizes possible. Now go a little further.

What happens when you have only one hand available to control the drafting and yarn formation? (The other hand must regulate the rate and direction of twist by controlling the drive wheel.) Well, that hand becomes very adept at fine tuning the flow of fibers through the fingers while regulating its own backward speed. Good fiber preparation becomes especially important, particularly if a smooth, strong yarn is required.

There's something else. The drafting hand has no choice but to continually pull the fiber supply away from the forming yarn; never are the fibers pulled out of the supply and fed into the twist. Thus it is the uninterrupted approaching twist that manages the smooth flow of fibers into year, helping to control size and uniformity. The result is a long, smooth, and relatively quick drafting of fibers, with the spinner observing the size, twist regularity, and consistency of a length of yarn before it is wound on.

Take another step down on the scale of tolls and technology and you reach the supported spindle. It is similar to the spindle wheel in that one hand is in control of the drafting, the wind-on procedure is a separate step, and the fiber supply must move in relation to the spun yarn. But here you have only the simplest of tools to work with, a stick and a weight, and you must rely almost solely upon the skills in your eyes and hands to produce a good yarn.

To get started on the support spindle, you go back to basics, learning to control each motion one at a time; twirl the spindle, stop it, draft the yarn to use up the twist. Until your spindle hand gets used to controlling the spindle at speed, this feels awkward and seems time-consuming. With practice, however, the motions of drafting the fibers and rotating the spindle become continuous, and later, surprisingly rapid. You cultivate a very sensitive touch in your drafting hand, smoothly controlling the flow of fibers ahead of the approaching twist, never pulling the spindle tip from its position or lifting the spindle from the ground. Your other hand learns complete control of the spindle, maximizing its speed and directing its energy into smooth rotation. Your hands work independently, yet in harmony. The resulting yarn flows directly from your acquired skills, independent of the influence of tool or machine.

Supported spindles are some of the simplest and oldest tools known. They have been used to make the finest natural-fiber fabrics known to man, still unmatched by machine or hand. They are used the world over by spinners whose livelihoods depend upon their yarns, and who rely upon the supported spindle for its combination of simplicity, efficiency, and portability.

By mastering this simple tool you'll find the fundamentals of yarn construction magnified, the consequences of inadequate fiber preparation clarified, and your dexterity and control more finely honed. Supported spindles can teach you, and through you, your students, the simple and far-reaching principle: good fibers + skillful control = superior yarn.

Lee Raven is the former editor of Spin-Off magazine.

December 1983

Spinning with a Supported Spindle

Lynn DeRose

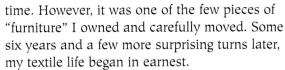

The first time I remember seeing someone spin, I was staying with a Berber family in the Sahara. Each night Mama spun while we sat about talking, joking, and generally entertaining ourselves, even though we did not share a common spoken language. I have a clear image of her spinning, using a spindle much the shape of my first drop spindle; however, she sat on the floor and used it supported.

I still have the impression that she would immediately fold a length of newly spun yarn back on itself, plying as she went along. With hindsight and more spinning knowledge, I am not sure, but think she was really showing me "the next step" before weaving.

After my visit, I fantasized returning to learn spinning and weaving from Mama. At that time I did not know that in their culture, spinning and weaving were tasks for married women only.

Some years later, a friend took a spinning  class and showed me the rudiments of spinning as she learned them herself. She later complained that everyone in her class got As but her. Maybe so, but the "average" skills she shared gave me a solid foundation. I loved spinning and worked on a drop spindle for quite some time, making enough yarn for my first handspun sweater, as I saved for a wheel.

After I finally acquired a wheel, life took me in unexpected directions and I did not use it often for a very long time. However, it was one of the few pieces of "furniture" I owned and carefully moved. Some six years and a few more surprising turns later, my textile life began in earnest.

At about this time, I overheard a quote attributed to Bette Hochberg: "Spin a pound of cotton on a supported spindle and you'll really know how to spin." Intrigued, I learned to spin with an African bead whorl from Mali and my interest in so-called primitive tools blossomed. What I learn from the necessarily focused drafting makes my wheel spinning both faster and more precise.

Now I am into my second pound of cotton, and in the home stretch on my first pound of wool spun on supported spindles, but I am not a purist. I delight in spinning on my wheels, and have no problem plying together or mixing in a project wheel-spun and spindle-spun yarns.

Working with handspindles, because of their portability, allows spinning to be an active part of my daily life even when I don't have time to sit at a wheel. I have two travel kits. One, inspired by pre-Columbian Peruvian workbaskets, is a relatively small seagrass basket containing fiber, several spindles, a few extra shafts and whorls, and a couple of support bowls. The other is a small square cloth bag with a shoulder strap, containing a handspindle or two and some cotton. I always carry one of these kits, and spin in what would otherwise be tedious times. I have spun thousands of yards while waiting . . . in medical offices, in airports, in lines of various kinds, on buses, in meetings or lectures, and even during conversations.

Watching me, other spinners often say, " . . . but I'm too impatient to spin that way." I'm too impatient not to. My fingers itch to twiddle, and those who know me well suggest I pick up my spinning if they want my full attention.

Supported spindle basics

A drop spindle is allowed to hang freely. Its weight tugs on the yarn being made, and that weight can be used to assist drafting. A supported spindle is supported by something—bowl, hand, foot, or ground. Its weight does not bear down on the yarn being spun. This makes it ideal for spinning very fine yarns or threads, because the newly drafted yarn need not be strong enough to support the weight of the spindle.

Supported handspindles, charkhas, and great or walking wheels all work on the same principle, called point spinning, which allows drafting without a strong tension or tug on the yarn. This drafting is easiest with short-stapled fibers such as cotton or cashmere, but I have seen admirable yarns spun on supported spindles from fine wools with 3- to 4-inch (7.5- to 10-cm) staples.

Point spinning is essentially a three-step process. Drafting is the first step. Next, the degree of twist needed to give the yarn stability and strength is inserted—*after* the fiber has been drafted. Finally, the yarn is wound onto the spindle shaft.

A supported spindle is a very simple tool. The most common type looks like a bead on a stick. Spinners have been making and using these tools for thousands of years, and they have been found at archaeological sites around the world. But despite the great numbers of prehistoric spindle whorls which have survived, there are remarkably few variations the world over. Photographs of whorls found in pre-Hispanic sites in Colombia are remarkably similar to those found in the various levels of Troy, and to some in my own collection that were purchased as "older" whorls from Mali in West Africa.

Although basically similar, there is variation among supported spindles. The shafts are usually wood or cane but can be metal, and can be pointed or have a hook at the top end. The whorls come in many shapes and sizes; they can be made of fired clay, wood, metal, or other materials; and they are positioned near the center of the shaft or toward the bottom end.

For example, the tiny, lightweight whorls found in pre-Hispanic Peruvian coastal sites are most often somewhat cone-shaped and weigh only a gram or so. These whorls were placed mid-shaft but slightly off-center in use; a complete spindle averaged about 10 to 12 inches (25 to 30 cm) in length, and with the whorl weighed a mere 5 to 7 grams (1/5–1/4 ounce). These lovely tools were exquisitely made and superbly balanced. My research suggests that these lightweight, centered-whorl spindles were supported by hand rather than twirled in a bowl.

Supported spindles are still in use today. My niece travels frequently to Central America and I always ask her to look for spinning tools. In Guatemala the most frequent response to her request was a somewhat dumbfounded look; the person questioned would direct her just to break a branch off a tree. Finally she did find what is commonly thought of as a Guatemalan cotton spindle, and I have since seen several for sale in this country. These spindles essentially consist of a dried mud ball on a stick, with a thin pitch coating over the whorl and lower portion of the stick. The whorl is an integral part of the spindle and cannot be removed. The two which I have weigh 37 grams and 43 grams (1 1/5–1 1/2 ounces).

One of my currently favorite spindles is a hand-supported cotton spindle from the Akha people in Southeast Asia, brought to me by a friend (see page 43). This type of spindle has a cane shaft approximately 8 to 10 inches (20 to 25 cm) long with a hook carved into one end. Centered on the shaft, the whorl is a flat disk 2 to 2 1/2 inches (5 to 6.5 cm) in diameter, made of a very dense wood, possibly mahogany. These spindles weigh from 10 to 30 grams (1/3–1 ounce). While weight may indicate use, it is also a highly personal preference. I prefer a small, light spindle. Other spinners enjoy working with heavier ones.

Making your own supported spindle

Traditionally, spinners have made their own spindles, and you can, too. To make a supported spindle, you'll need a bead for the whorl, a dowel for the shaft, and a pencil sharpener and an

Xacto-type knife for sharpening and shaping the dowel.

The bead or whorl. I have whorls in many shapes and sizes—cones, spheres, half-spheres, and some that remind me of tiny flying saucers. My favorites come from the Mopti area in Mali, where they were originally used for both cotton and wool. These whorls weigh between 12 and 18 grams (.4–.6 ounce) and are half-spheres of a black-slipped, baked clay, decorated with a variety of incised designs that all include little white circles as part of the pattern.[2]

Some years ago whorls from West Africa were fairly common in bead and ethnic art shops. They were frequently strung on coarse twine and sold as primitive necklaces. Now they are becoming increasingly rare. I've asked around, and it seems that importers are unable to locate them. But a few are still out there . . . I hear occasional-ly from a gleeful student or friend who has found an African whorl in a bead shop.

The whorls shown in Frederick Shaffer's *Indian Designs from Ancient Ecuador* are similar in shape and use to the better-known Peruvian ones. Currently a rough-baked clay copy of the Ecuadoran whorls can sometimes be found in bead stores. These modern replications are cheap, but you may have to purchase several to find a well-balanced one that doesn't crumble from the pressure of being pushed onto a shaft. For these whorls, where the hole is quite small, an unmodified bamboo skewer can serve quite nicely as a spindle shaft. (I don't usually recommend bamboo shafts, though, because they tend to splinter when shaped.)

If you can't find a true whorl, don't despair. To some degree, the difference between a bead and a whorl is academic. For instance, the hole through a whorl tends to be tapered, being slightly larger at the bottom than on top, whereas the holes in most modern beads are a consistent diameter for their entire length. But if a bead is well balanced, has a relatively large, well-centered hole, and pleases your eye, it could easily become a whorl for you.

Among the beads I have converted to whorls is a large, amber bead that weighs about 25 grams (.9 ounce) and is a dream to spin with. At the other end of the weight scale, I have a small, 3.5-gram (.1-ounce) onyx bead that is just right for other moods and other fibers. I enjoy using my amber spindle for longer-stapled fibers, and the lighter spindles for fibers with shorter staples. (As a rule of thumb, the heavier the spindle, the slower the rotation; the slower the rotation, the easier it is to draft longer fibers.)

I've been very specific about the weights of my whorls, but if you don't have access to a small scale, simply heft the bead you're considering in your hand and begin building a memory for the comparative feel of the weight you prefer. Remembering that specific weight choices are

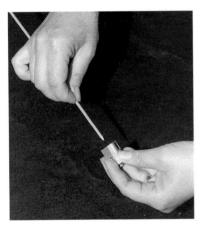

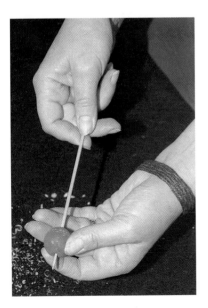

You can make your own supported spindle, using a bead for the whorl and a piece of ⅛-inch hardwood dowel for the shaft. Sharpen the end of the dowel with a pencil sharpener, then taper the tip by shaving it with a sharp knife until you can slide the bead snugly into place, about 1 to 1½ inches from the bottom end of the shaft.

2 *A potter who lives near me now, but is originally from Mali, was very excited to see me spinning with this familiar tool. But he asked about my storytelling, not my spinning. In Mali, "spinning a yarn" is not just a cliché; a spinner gathers children to hear stories as she sits and spins.*

extremely personal preferences, here is a guide. Traditionally, most whorls weigh under 30 grams (about 1 ounce), and a complete spindle weighs well under 45 grams (1½ ounces). Whorls weighing between 12 and 18 grams feel comfortable to most spinners, but you may find that whorls weighing only 3 to 7 grams feel uncomfortably light until the weight of the cop (the wound-on yarn) begins to help with the work. (You can always double the whorls, removing one when the cop is large enough to be a consideration.) How often you spin with your supported spindle and how long you work in a single session will influence your choice of weight and whorl shape.

Lightweight beads tend to be small, or are made of relatively porous materials such as wood, bone, or Fimo. When gently tossed in your

Set the bottom of the spindle in a shallow cup on the floor in front of you, let your twirling arm rest comfortably at your side, and grip the shaft where your fingers reach it. This is your "natural reach." Cut off the top of the dowel about 1 inch above that point. Now sharpen the top of the dowel with a pencil sharpener; shave it with a sharp knife to give it a thinner, slightly faceted profile; and finally, trim off the tip at a 45° angle to reduce the "popping" that happens each time the turning of the spindle puts another twist into the yarn.

palm, the sensation of something being in your hand will probably dominate over any feeling of weight. I usually prefer whorls made of denser materials, such as stone, clay, or glass, but I am always willing to be surprised. I carry a shaft and some wadding when investigating bead stores. If you don't have a shaft, try spinning a bead like a top on a counter to check for balance. Mistakes? Yes, I have a collection of would-be whorls, but they are still functional, attractive beads that some day will make a necklace or two.

The shaft. A spindle shaft can easily be made from a ⅛-inch (3-mm) hardwood dowel. Cut the standard 36-inch (90-cm) length into thirds. (You can try breaking it, but without deep scoring dowels rarely break cleanly.) Take one of these 12-inch (30-cm) lengths and sharpen one tip with a pencil sharpener, then, while rotating the dowel in your hands, start shaving the sharpened tip into a tapered point using an Xacto-style knife. Be patient and keep the knife blade relatively flat, to avoid gouging or splintering the wood. This will be the bottom end of the spindle. Gradually lengthen the taper until you can slip your whorl snugly onto the shaft. The bottom tip should project about 1 to 1½ inches (2.5 to 4 cm) through the whorl. If you get a bit exuberant with your shaving don't worry; you can always make minor adjustments with a little bit of cotton or wool wadding.

To shape the spinning tip, sit on the floor and place the spindle vertically in front of you. Use your drafting hand (the one that holds the fiber) to hold the whorl end against the floor. Grasp the top with your other hand (the hand that will twirl the spindle), using your "natural reach." To do this, allow your non-drafting arm to hang at rest. Now keep your shoulder and upper arm relaxed, but lift your forearm at the elbow and grasp the dowel with your thumb and forefinger. This position is your natural reach. Most spinners find that if their elbow is somewhere near their waist, their forearm can be pivoted with minimum effort and used for extended periods without discomfort. I cannot stress this enough: *your arm and shoulder should be relaxed and comfortable.* Eventually you may want to have them in this position for long stretches of time. Grasp the shaft several times until you're sure your shoulder isn't hunching

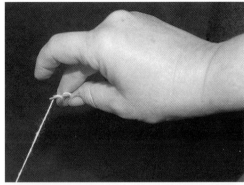

Here's a spinner's-eye view of the top of the spindle. Using the hand that you write with, spin the spindle by rolling it between your middle finger and thumb, like you would snap your fingers. Then catch the shaft and let it twirl freely in the space between your bent fingers and thumb.

up. Mark where your fingers are touching the dowel, then cut off the top of the dowel about 1 inch (2.5 cm) above the mark.

Sharpen this tip with your pencil sharpener. You can choose to be finished at this point, but with some additional shaping your spindle will be more comfortable and efficient. Shave this top end to a taper, much as you did for the whorl end. This tapering serves several functions. A slightly faceted profile offers a surface that transfers energy from fingers to spindle without as much slippage as you'll experience with a smooth surface. The smaller tip also gains you a few more twists per finger-snap than the full circumference of the dowel (it's like using a smaller flyer whorl on your wheel). It will also transfer less stress to the fragile, pre-thread, drafted fiber because the "pop" off the top will be less violent (this is similar to the effect of a small orifice size on a wheel).

Be sure the whorl is snug on the shaft, then give it a test whirl. If the spindle seems off-balance, try rotating the whorl by small increments. If you still can't balance the spindle, try putting the whorl on the other end of the shaft. Once you have found the best balance, you can put the finishing touch on the shaft. Clip the very tip of the drafting end so it has a 45° profile. This tends to decrease the "pop" vibration even more.

Try to avoid gluing the whorl to the shaft. Doing so limits your options. Shafts break, whorls split, and sometimes you need to slip off a cop. If you can remove the whorl, you can

slide the cop down off the tapered bottom end of the shaft.

The support bowl. You'll need a shallow container to keep the bottom of your spindle from skidding away. I have a collection of support bowls that includes crystal and wooden salt cellars; gourd spoons from Africa, Russia, and Mexico; ceramic sake cups; and even a wooden egg cup. Almost anything will do; I've even used the inner heel of my shoe in a pinch. Different bowls work for different whorls and different spinners. If it works for you, use it.

My favorite support bowl is a small wooden bowl which was identified to me as an Indian butter bowl. I like it for several reasons. First, it's quiet. Some combinations of bowls and spindles make very irritating sounds. Heard once or twice, such noise can be ignored, but heard frequently it will set your teeth on edge and you'll stop spinning. Although small, this bowl is stable, with

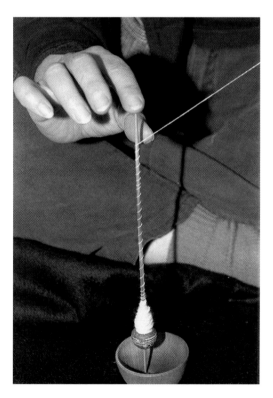

Turn the spindle in the same direction to wind on the yarn as you turn it for spinning. In this photo, Lynn is turning the spindle clockwise to make Z-twist yarn. The leader "candy canes" up the shaft and is held out at about a 45° angle. That angle is important. If you hold the yarn too low, it will start winding around the shaft; if you lift it too high, it will slip right off the end of the shaft.

most of its weight in the base. The lip is open and shallow, so my whorls rarely bang against it. The very rounded interior has a small dimple at the bottom, which allows the spindle to slide quickly to a central point and focuses the spinning energy. Finally, I very much enjoy both the look and the feel of this little bowl.

Spinning with a supported spindle

When you have a spindle and bowl, you're ready to try spinning. Refer to the photos and captions as you read through the text below. Sit on the floor or in a chair, wherever you're comfortable. Practice spinning the spindle by snapping it between your thumb and middle finger, then catching it and letting it twirl in the space between your bent fingers and thumb. Different spinners have different ways of doing this. It doesn't really matter how you use your fingers, as long as you can give a fast twist to the spindle, hold the shaft so it rotates freely without wobbling, and stop it quickly when you want to.

You will need to tie on a leader or make your own. For the shortcut, just tie a fine thread to the base of the shaft, near the whorl. To make your own leader, moisten the tip of your spindle enough to attach the end of your fiber source (a little spit does the trick). With the fiber caught onto the tip, twist the spindle and draft a length of yarn. Push it down near the whorl and wrap it around a few times to secure it there, then spiral it up the shaft like any other leader. This impromptu leader can be quite irregular, as long as it is twisted enough to be stable. Hold the leader at a 45° angle from the top of the shaft. It will "pop" off the tip of the shaft with each revolution of the spindle, creating the twist that travels up the yarn.

Spinning with a supported spindle feels very different from spinning on a wheel, because there is no tension—and very little twist in the yarn as you draft. While you're drafting, the yarn will feel very soft and weak. Hold the fiber gently and move your arm slowly. Spin the spindle and catch it, then draft, draft, draft. For each snap of the spindle, continue to draft until you see no twist at all in the drafting zone. Then twirl the spindle again.

Remember that you are in complete control of the twist with one hand and of drafting with the other. Learning to use a supported spindle is a matter of learning to coordinate the two. Stay completely focused on the drafting triangle. If the fibers start to drift apart, slow down your drafting or increase your twisting. Conversely, if drafting is a struggle, the twist has gotten into your fiber supply, so you have to speed up your drafting or slow down your twisting.

When you've drafted a full arm's length, pinch off the yarn and keep rotating the spindle to add the final amount of twist. As you add twist, it will feel like the yarn is getting subtly shorter. This isn't anything you can measure, but it's a very definite feeling that you can tune in to. I judge final twist by the feeling of this "draw-up" and/or by counting the number of additional times I spin the spindle.

As you wind the yarn onto the shaft, try to keep the cop close to the whorl. Generally, the shorter, tighter, and more compact the cop, the easier it is to remove or wind off. Keep adding

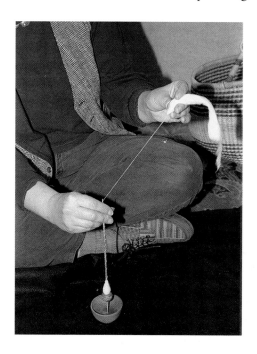

As you start to spin, the rhythm is: Spin. Catch. Draft, draft, draft. Spin. Catch. Draft, draft, draft. For each snap of the spin, continue drafting until you have used up all the twist inserted by your spin and the yarn is on the verge of slipping apart. Hold the fiber loosely and draft slowly and gently. Relax and let your fingers feel what is happening.

When your arm is fully extended, pinch off the yarn and insert enough twist to stabilize it. As you add twist, it feels like the yarn is getting shorter. Pay attention to this feeling, and you can use it to judge when the yarn is twisted enough to wind on. Or, you can count how many additional times you twirl the spindle. For example, Lynn is adding six more twirls of the spindle to each arm's length of this fine cotton yarn.

yarn until the spindle is too heavy to spin comfortably or is awkward to wind.

A neat cop can be slipped off the spindle stick and placed on another small stick for storage, plying, or unwinding. Shish kabob skewers or knitting needles (size 1—2.5 mm—or smaller) are good for this purpose. Often a paper quill is wound on a great wheel's spindle to provide the cop with ready-made storage. This idea can be adapted to many supported spindles.

If you want to ply the yarn directly from two or more supported spindles, you can stick the shafts through holes punched in the sides of a shoebox. Then set the shoebox on edge, so the shafts are vertical, not horizontal—that puts less stress on the yarn as you unwind it. You could ply with the supported spindle itself (just twirl it in the opposite direction), but I rarely do. I usually wind the yarn off onto bobbins and ply with my wheel.

Lynn DeRose, of Portland, Oregon, received a Lee Kirschner-Lewis study grant from the Northwest Regional Spinner's Association to pursue her interest in the history and practical use of Peruvian supported spindles.

Photo credit: Rita Buchanan

When the yarn is twisted enough, lift the spindle out of the support bowl and hold it horizontally in your hand. Pull on the yarn to unwind the "candy cane," then twirl the spindle to wind on the yarn.

Resources

Barber, E. J. W. *Prehistoric Textiles*. Princeton: Princeton University Press, 1991.

Enciso, Jorge. Designs From Pre-Columbian Mexico. New York: Dover, 1971. This is easy to confuse with Enciso's other book, *Design Motifs from Ancient Mexico*, which pictures designs from cylinder seals. The book you want consists of designs from Melacates (spindle whorls).

Hochberg, Bette. *Handspindles*. Santa Cruz, California: Bette and Bernard Hochberg, 1977. Distributed by Straw Into Gold, Berkeley, California.

————. "Spinning With A Bead Whorl Spindle." In *Reprints of Bette Hochberg's Articles*. Santa Cruz, California: Bette and Bernard Hochberg, 1982.

Labbe, Armand J. *Colombia Before Columbus*. New York: Rizzoli, 1986. Page 100.

Liu, Robert K. "Spindle Whorls, Part I: Some Comments and Speculations." *The Bead Journal 3* (1978): pages 87–103. This is the standard reference work on the difference between spindle whorls and beads.

Shaffer, Frederick W. *Indian Designs from Ancient Ecuador*. New York: Dover, 1979.

Spring 1995

Akha Spinning

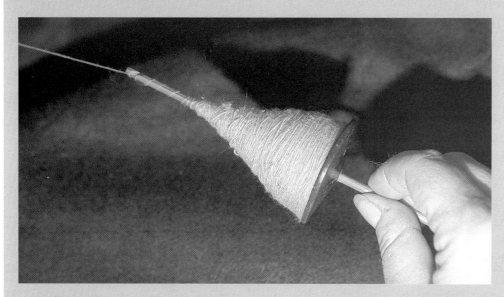

There are various forms of supported spindles. This type is used by the Akha people in Southeast Asia for spinning cotton. The whorl is a flat wooden disk located just below mid-shaft. There's a hook carved into the top of the shaft.

To use the Akha spindle, Lynn DeRose supports and twirls the shaft with her right hand, and drafts straight away from the tip. Watching her spin this way is like watching a butterfly raise and lower its wings. Her hands and arms reach out to both sides as she drafts and twists the yarn, then come back together again as she winds the yarn onto the spindle. Back and forth, back and forth, she spins and winds on. It's a calm and soothing gesture.

Spinning on a Takli Spindle

Celia Quinn

A takli is a particular kind of supported spindle that comes from India. It has a brass whorl about the size of a nickel, and an iron shaft about 8 inches (20 cm) long that's shaped into a flat hook at the top end. Taklis are lightweight—they usually weigh about ½ ounce (14 grams)—and when you twirl them, they spin very fast and keep spinning for a long time. This makes them ideal for spinning fine yarns.

Right now, it's hard to buy an Indian-made takli in the United States; most suppliers have sold out their inventories, and it's taking a long time for replacement orders to come in. But many spinners already have a takli tucked away, because they were abundant and inexpensive a few years ago. If you have one that you acquired at a workshop, conference, or shop at one time or another, get it out now and give it another try, or share it with other spinners in your guild. If you don't have one, you can substitute. A few suppliers now offer some beautiful takli-like spindles made by American craftworkers, with metal or glass whorls and thin metal shafts that curve into a graceful hook on top.

A takli is used as a supported spindle. I usually set mine in a little bowl made of gourd rind or just twirl it on my jeans. Some spinners drape a square of leather or canvas over their thigh; that makes a non-skid surface and protects their leg from the sharp end of the spindle.

After you've gotten used to

If you like sitting on the floor or ground, you can support the bottom end of the takli in a shallow container. This bowl is made from a gourd rind; the inside is just rough enough to keep the takli from skidding.

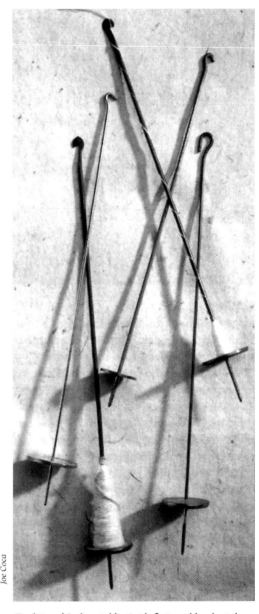

Joe Coca

Traditional Indian taklis (with flattened hook at the top) and handmade American taklis by Henry M. Edwards III, some with coin whorls. All are nicely balanced.

using a takli, I think the most comfortable position is to hold the spindle at your side and draft off the tip at a 45° angle, but for beginners, I recommend starting with the spindle in a vertical position and drafting straight up. You can sit in a chair or on the floor. Hold the spindle upright on a non-skid surface and give it a twirl. It should spin steadily, with no vibration or wobbling. Take a minute to practice twirling the takli before you start to spin. Turn it clockwise to make Z-twist yarn. Flick the shaft with your thumb, then let it tilt just enough to fall into the notch where your fingers bend. Cradle it there and let it glide. With practice, this flick, catch, and glide will become a smooth, continuous gesture.

If you want to spin cotton, I recommend that you use an Upland or acala cotton rather than pima cotton, and choose a carded rather than combed preparation. It's often easier to draft from one end of a cotton sliver than the other; try both ends to see if you can tell the difference. You can make your own leader by pulling out a wisp of fibers and twisting it between your hands or against your thigh, or just find some thin yarn and use that.

Slowly turn the spindle clockwise and hold the yarn taut as you wrap the leader around the shaft. Make several turns near the whorl, then spiral up the shaft, and make a few horizontal wraps close together just under the hook. Leave about 2 inches (5 cm) of yarn above the hook.

At first, it helps to break the spinning process into separate steps. Twirl the spindle and let it drop into your bent fingers and glide briefly. Then stop it and hold it in place. With your other hand gently holding the fiber right near the drafting triangle (remember: hold close but loose), draft a few inches up away from the spindle. Watch what's happening, and stop drafting as soon as the yarn starts to thin out. Pinch with your fingers so the twist can't run up into the fiber supply.

Now try it again. Twirl the spindle. Stop the spindle. Relax your fingers and draw out some yarn. Pinch down with your fingers and twirl again. Talking to yourself helps establish the sequence: twirl, stop, relax, draw; twirl, stop, relax, draw. With practice, the pace accelerates, both hands work together, and the rhythm becomes, twirl, draw! twirl, draw!

You probably won't have to remind yourself

Celia Quinn demonstrates takli spinning at workshops and conferences around the country. Here she is sitting in a chair, twirling the takli on her leg, and drafting at a 45° angle from the tip of the spindle to spin a fine cotton yarn. One hand twirls and supports the spindle, and the other hand holds the fiber and draws out the yarn. Notice how Celia has the cotton sliver wrapped around a distaff that hangs from her wrist. That's a handy way to keep the fiber supply organized and out of the way.

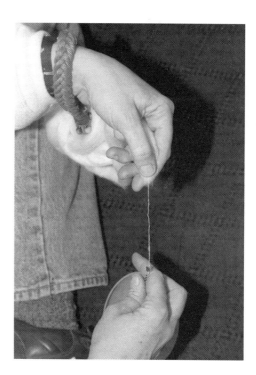

When you're first learning to use a takli, it's easiest if you hold the spindle vertically and draft straight up. Twirl the spindle, then catch and hold it. Gently hold the fiber close to the drafting zone, and draw up until the yarn starts to get thin, then stop drafting and twist again. Take a close look at this picture to see how Celia has flattened the fiber between her thumb and first finger. That little triangle where the fibers pull down into the yarn is the drafting zone.

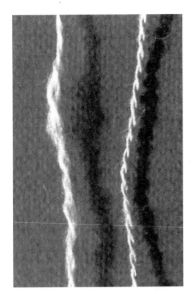

As you're drafting on the takli, there's very little twist in the yarn. Doubled back on itself, it looks like the sample on the left. After drafting an arm's length, you keep twirling the spindle to add extra twist. When it's ready to wind on, a doubled-back section of the yarn looks like the sample on the right.

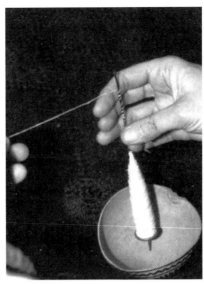

Turn the spindle in the same direction to wind on the yarn as you turn it for spinning. Hold the yarn taut as you spiral up the shaft, and make a few extra wraps right under the hook. If you wind your yarn into a firm neat cone, your spindle will hold more yarn, and you'll have an easier time winding it off into a skein.

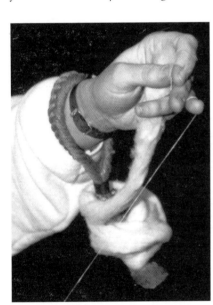

Fluent spindle-spinners have nifty ways of using their fingers to regulate twist and prevent tangles. Take a look at how Celia has wrapped the yarn around her little finger. She does that to keep the twist from running up to the fiber supply as she builds up the final twist in the yarn and winds it onto the spindle.

to pinch down on the fiber supply. The challenge for most spinners is learning to relax and let go of the fiber enough to draft it. It also takes a while to get used to the feeling of drafting with so little twist in the yarn. With a supported spindle like a takli, you first draw out the yarn as far as your arm can comfortably reach; the yarn at this stage is still very weak, because it has very low twist. Then, after you've drafted a length of yarn, you add extra twist to give it strength. You can tell when you've added enough twist by pulling the yarn between your hands and feeling its strength, or by letting it double back on itself and looking at it.

Resist the temptation to use both hands near the drafting zone. Make them work separately—one to twirl the spindle, the other to hold the fiber. If you try to use the takli like a drop spindle, moving one hand back and forth from the spindle to the

drafting zone, you'll never get up to speed and take advantage of its full potential.

When you've drafted and twisted an arm's length of yarn, lower your arm until it's perpendicular to the spindle. Let the spindle fall into that notched place in your fingers, and pull gently on the yarn to unwind it down the shaft; the spindle will turn "backwards" as the yarn unwinds. Then, still holding the yarn off to the side, twirl the spindle in the spinning direction to wind on the yarn. Hold the yarn taut as you wind on, and try to build it up into a neat, firm cone. Spiral the yarn up the shaft, remembering to make a few horizontal wraps just under the hook, and start twirling and drafting again.

If you're careful about winding it on, you can pack a lot of yarn onto a takli. When mine is full, I make the yarn into a skein by hanging onto the hook end of the shaft and holding the takli parallel to the ground as my arm swings up, over, and around my niddy noddy. If you prefer to use a skein reel, you could hold the takli with one hand as you slowly turn the reel. Either way, with one skein finished, you're ready to spin some more!

Celia Quinn has spun the very finest contemporary cotton yarn anybody around here has ever seen. She lives in Alaska, but travels to give workshops.

American-crafted taklis, by Henry M. Edwards III, are available from The Wool Room (catalog is $1 from The Wool Room, Joe's Hill Road, Brewster, New York 10509).

Indian taklis are available from Celia Quinn, PO Box 1808, Homer, Alaska 99603.

Photo credit: Rita Buchanan

Spring 1995

Chapter Four

MAKE YOUR OWN
HANDSPINDLE AND DISTAFF

Handspinners are known for the creative urge.
For many, this urge extends to making tools. These
articles offer a diverse lot of handspindle designs
from the simplest hooked stick (in Chapter One)
to a high-tech CD handspindle. And when it comes
to the distaff, even more alternatives are offered,
again from the very simple stick in several configu-
rations to the most elegant bracelet styles. And for
those who want to extend the use of their favorite
spindle, we offer instruction on making and using
paper quills.

Spindles in an Evening

Amy S. Durgeloh

I was one of many who learned to spin on a handspindle and then literally dropped it when I got my first wheel. After all, that drop spindle was heavy and slow, and I couldn't spin anything on it but medium- to heavy-weight wool. When *Spin·Off* featured spindle spinning in Spring 1995, I was spurred to reconsider the handspindle. People were using small, lightweight spindles and spinning lovely, fine yarn on them!

At the time, I was living on an island in the Bering Sea, two hundred miles from the Alaska coast. As you can imagine, there were no fiber stores. I decided to make a light spindle. From the available materials, I made a high-whorl drop spindle which is poorly balanced, although I've learned that high-whorl spindles are quite forgiving. I have spun many miles of yarn on this crude, wobbly thing.

But I wanted a better balanced, lighter, and more attractive spindle. It occurred to me that I could use the toy wooden wheels which are sold in craft stores to provide me with whorls. One evening I made several spindles, using 1¼-inch and 1½-inch (3- and 3.8-cm) wheels, dowels, screw hooks, and a little wood glue. They are wonderful!

The toy wheels have good balance and the finished spindles weigh only about ⅓ to ½ ounce (9.5 to 14 g). My cost has averaged $1.75 per spindle. I've spun cotton, linen, dog, and silk on these tools.

I have not abandoned my wheel. It still holds a place of honor in the living room. But my spindles are great for portable projects, and they help me meet so many interesting people. What do you do on your lunch break?

Amy S. Durgeloh lives in Anchorage, Alaska, and makes good use of her spare moments at work and at home. . .

Winter 98

With dowels, small cup hooks, and toy wheels from a craft store, Amy Durgeloh finds she can make spindles by the handful for a minimal investment of money and time.

Making Clay Spindle Whorls

JL Spradley

The spindle whorls found in archaeological sites were reworked from broken pottery. The modern spinner who attempts to rework the dinner plate she or he broke last will be in for a surprise, however, for Indian pottery was fired at lower temperatures than modern china and stoneware. Hence, it was soft and well suited to reworking. Modern china and stoneware are fired at high temperatures, and will crack at the slightest error on the part of the whorl-maker. It is far less frustrating to begin with a softer material. I have found that the orange clay saucers designed for plant pots are ideal for the beginning whorl-maker. They are available at most supermarkets and plant stores.

The saucers come in various sizes. Purchase saucers with bottoms slightly bigger than the size of the intended whorl. It is best to have several on hand, in case you break one while working with it. The size of a spindle whorl is largely dependent on the type of yarn you intend to spin and on your method of spinning. If you are spinning wool or other animal hair, a large spindle whorl is in order because of the bulk of the yarn. Cotton, linen, or silk thread will require a smaller whorl. Drop spinning requires a heavier whorl than Navajo-style spinning. Evaluate your needs and plan the whorl accordingly.

When you have determined the size of your whorl, the size of the shaft follows logically. The smaller the whorl, the smaller the shaft. Shaft sizes usually range from one centimeter to four or five millimeters, the smallest used for spinning fine thread. Dowel sticks, available at hardware and lumber stores, make excellent shafts.

Before you make your whorl, you will need to prepare the shaft. The length of the shaft depends entirely on your own personal preferences. If you have a spindle that seems perfect to you, cut your dowel to the length of the shaft of that spindle. If your usual spindle's shaft seems a little too short or too long, adjust the length of the dowel for your new spindle accordingly.

Putting a point on the bottom of your shaft is easily accomplished with an ordinary pencil sharpener and sandpaper for smoothness. If you like a notch at the top of your spindle, cut one with a coping saw. If you prefer a groove around the top, the same coping saw can be used to cut one. You will want to sand your shaft carefully, so no rough edges can snag your yarn.

Once the shaft is prepared, set it aside and pick up a saucer. If you turn the saucer over, you will see that the sides of the saucer slope outward from the base. It is the base of the saucer that will form your whorl. Using a ruler, measure the diameter of the base and find the

A clay plant pot saucer is an ideal first project.

Holding the saucer on its side, cut the rim from the base.

Smooth the edges of the saucer with a file.

Using an ordinary drill bit, bore a hole through the center.

The tools you will need.

The completed whorl.

The completed spindle.

center. Mark this spot with a pencil. Now mark a circle the size of your desired whorl with a compass.

The clay of the saucer will be soft enough to cut with a keyhole or coping saw, so the first step is to remove the sides of the saucer. Tip the saucer onto its edge and hold it firmly. Using your saw, cut straight through the saucer near the base. Don't try to rush this cut, because too much pressure will crack the base. Once the cut is completed, you are left with the base and clay ring that composed the sides of the saucer. Using a file or coarse sandpaper, file the base down to the circle you marked previously. Again, don't try to hurry this or the whorl may crack.

Once the outside of the whorl has been smoothed, you will need to make the center hole for the shaft. It is possible to drill a hole in the whorl using an electric drill. This method often cracks the whorl, however. A slower, but safer, method is to bore the hole by hand. Pad your palm with a piece of leather, or several layers of cloth. Then, using a commercial drill bit slightly smaller than your shaft, bore a hole through the center of the whorl, using a screwing, back and forth movement. Do not press down hard on the whorl or it will crack. Once the initial hole is made, enlarge it with sandpaper or a round file, checking it carefully for fit. The shaft should fit snugly through the hole. The whorl should not fall off if you shake the spindle or when you apply gentle pressure. If you happen to make the whorl center too large, you can glue supports to the shaft underneath the whorl to keep it from slipping off.

If you wish to decorate the whorl, tempra or acrylic paints work well on clay. Be sure to use a craft fixative or lacquer over the paint to protect the yarn from staining.

The process for making spindle whorls from china or stoneware is the same as for clay, but if you want to try it, you must be much more patient, for these materials crack at the slightest excess pressure.

Once you've completed your spindle, spin some yarn or thread and see how you like using a personal spindle created by the spinner—you.

Spring 1983

CD Spindles

Melissa Croci

I would like to start by saying that the idea for a spindle made from compact disks (CDs) is not original to me. I first heard about it from postings on the Spindlitis Net (spindle@xws.com), run by Teri Pittman (www.xws.com/terispage/spindle.html). For more good thoughts about spindle spinning, come join the group![1] The CD spindle is very easy to build and can be made as a top-whorl (my preference) or a bottom-whorl spindle.

Materials and tools

Except for the CDs (I use the free ones that arrive in the mail), all the materials can be found at a good hardware store.

- two CDs
- 1 hardwood dowel, $\frac{5}{16}$ inch or $\frac{3}{8}$ inch (8 mm or 9.5 mm) in diameter and 12 inches (30 cm) long (use the larger-diameter dowel if you want a spindle with a thicker shaft)
- 1 rubber gasket, inner diameter $\frac{3}{8}$ inch (9.5 mm) and outer diameter $\frac{3}{4}$ inch (19 mm): only needed if you're using $\frac{5}{16}$-inch (8-mm) dowel; may also be found at Radio Shack or other electronics suppliers
- 1 piece of poly tubing, inner diameter $\frac{5}{16}$-inch (8 mm) and outer diameter $\frac{3}{8}$ inch (9.5 mm), 1 inch (2.5 cm) long
- 1 small cup hook (optional)
- small saw or pruning shears (to trim spindle shaft and make optional notch)

---

[1] Editor's note: Will the originator of this idea please stand up? We'd love to know who came up with this marvelous and thrifty tool, and to acknowledge their ingenuity.

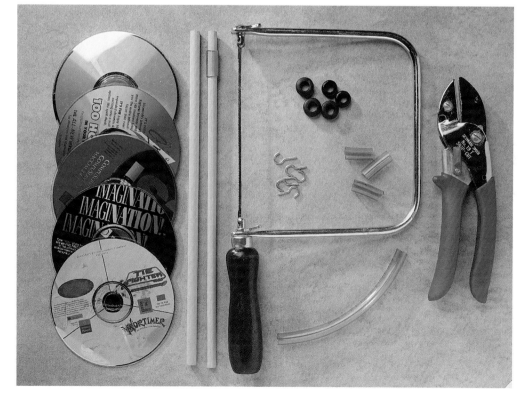

Outdated or duplicate CDs can be turned into efficient spindles. Here are the necessary supplies and tools. Black rubber gaskets are used to reduce the size of the CDs' center holes so the dowel will pressure-fit in place. The clear plastic tubing is needed only if you're using the thinner dowel, and serves as a spacer for the section of dowel which fits into the rubber gasket. Hooks are optional; you can carve a hook shape into one end of the dowel. A lightweight saw or pruner handles all the cutting involved; sturdy scissors work best on the plastic tubing.

Assembly

Step 1. Hold the two CDs together and insert the gasket into the aligned holes in the centers of the CDs.

Step 2 for ⅜ -inch (9.5-mm) dowel. Insert the 12-inch dowel into the center hole of the gasket.

Step 2 for 5⁄16-inch (8-mm) dowel. Slide the 1-inch (2.5 cm) length of poly tubing onto the 12-inch (30-cm) dowel so the tubing's end is about ¼ inch (6 mm) from one end of the dowel. Insert the end of the dowel with the tubing into the center hole of the gasket.[2]

---

[2] Editor's note: Our tubing wasn't precisely the right size, so we found we had to put the tubing into the gasket, then insert the gasket into the CDs, and finally work the shaft of the dowel into the tubing.

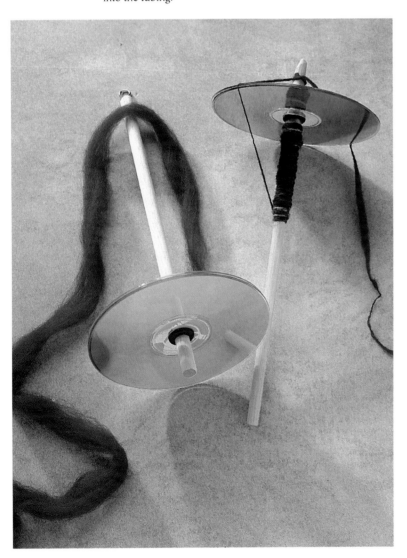

Step 2 notes for both sizes of dowel. The rubber gasket should provide a secure grip on the dowel. One end of the dowel should protrude about 1 inch (2.5 cm) from one side of the CDs; the long shaft of about 11 inches (28 cm) will protrude from the other side. (Precise placement of the dowel can be adjusted later to suit your preferences.)

Step 3. If you prefer a top-whorl spindle, screw the cup hook into the shorter end of the dowel. If you prefer a bottom-whorl spindle, screw the cup hook into the longer end of the dowel. Making a pilot hole with a fine drill bit can facilitate this task. For really fine cup hooks, it isn't necessary. For slightly coarser hooks, the pilot hole can prevent the end of the dowel from splitting.

If you prefer a notched spindle, omit the cup hook and cut a small notch in the end of the dowel.

Step 4. Adjust the length of the spindle shaft to your preferences by trimming the dowel. All mine end up about 10 inches (25.5 cm) long.

Melissa Croci, of Groveland, California, has been spinning for five years, and started on spindles when Spin·Off published an issue featuring them (Spring 1995). She credits her husband, Carl, with expediting construction of her first CD spindle, and her Angora rabbits and two cats for helping with fiber production.

Spring 1999

Spindles can be bottom-whorl or top-whorl. The bottom-whorl spindle, on the left, uses the larger-diameter dowel for its shaft and has a cup hook at the top. The top-whorl spindle, on the right, was made with the smaller-diameter dowel and a plastic spacer. The carved hook at its top was rough-shaped with the saw and then sanded smooth.

Paper Quills for Spindle Spinning

Marna Mackay

Paper quills can be very handy when you're spinning on a great wheel, a quill spindle, or a drop spindle. Put a quill in place before you start to spin and you can empty the spindle without winding off—just remove the quill. Full quills can be stored on a lazy kate for future handling.

Make several quills while you're at it. You will need: cardboard (empty cereal box–weight is perfect), letterweight paper, water-soluble glue, transparent tape, scissors.

On a piece of cardboard, trace and cut out a circle with a diameter of about 2½ inches (6.25 cm). Make sure the center hole is marked.

On a piece of letterweight paper, draw and cut out a rectangle that measures 1⅞ by 4⅝ inches (4.7 × 11.7 cm).

Position the rectangle lengthwise along the spindle you plan to use, wrap the paper tightly around the shaft, and glue down the edges. Quickly remove any excess glue from the spindle (a damp paper towel works, or you may want to wrap the spindle in plastic wrap before adding

the rectangle). Transparent tape can help fasten the edges, but do not wrap the ends of the tube with tape. Allow the tube to dry.

With the scissors, enlarge the marked center hole on the cardboard disk so that the paper tube fits into it snugly. Push the disk down over the tube, allowing ¼ inch (6 mm) to protrude at the bottom. Snip four evenly spaced cuts around the protruding section. Bend over these snipped tabs

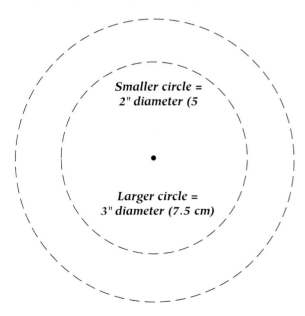

Smaller circle = 2" diameter (5

Larger circle = 3" diameter (7.5 cm)

A quill slides over a spindle shaft and serves as a "bobbin" for spindle-spun yarn.

and glue them to the disk. When the glue dries, your quill is ready.

If you don't have a lazy kate, you can easily make a useful quill holder from a block of wood 1–2 inches (2.5–5 cm) thick, 7–8 inches (17.8–20.3 cm) long, and about 5 inches (13 cm) wide. Oak works well because it's heavy enough to be stable.

Drill two ¼-inch (6-mm) holes in the board, about 4¹⁄₁₆ inches (10.2 cm) apart. Make certain the holes are equidistant from the edges of the board. Push a pair of size 9 (6 mm) knitting needles through the holes, and set the block down so it rests on the heads of the needles. If the size 9 needles are too large for your quill, use a smaller needle that will fit. The quills need to fit loosely on their supports, so they will turn easily. Presto!

If a quill tends to fly off the top of the needle, wrap a rubber band around the needle's tip or prop the block so the needles point slightly away from you and the yarn unwinds from the side of the quill.

There are many ways to improve on these ideas and you may want to alter the measurements to fit your particular needs, but this will get you started.

Marna Mackay, of Covington, Pennsylvania, has used quills for quite a while on her great wheel. One day, for amusement, she made one for a drop spindle. It was fun and expanded her use of the spindle.

Spring 1995

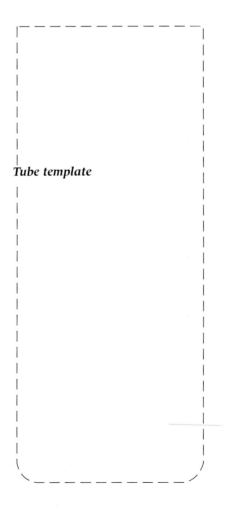

Tube template

Simple Distaffs

Rita Buchanan

For many spinners, one of the challenges of using a handspindle is figuring out how to hold the fiber. You want to be able to hold enough fiber that you can spin continually without frequent interruptions to pick up more fiber and make a join, but you don't want the fiber to become a nuisance by flopping around or catching onto the yarn.

Distaffs are the answer to this problem. They provide a way to hold a spindle's worth of fiber and keep it neatly organized and out of your way.

Traditional spinners relied on distaffs, but many contemporary spinners overlook these nifty tools.

There are several styles of distaffs. Which type makes you happy depends on the kind of fiber you're spinning and your hand position. Something's wrong if the distaff seems awkward or intrusive, if you feel strain or tension in your hand, or if you have trouble controlling the drafting zone. If you get frustrated, stop. Then try again, using a dif-

A hand-held stick distaff can be used with a handspindle or a wheel.

ferent tool or technique. When you've made the right match, you're hardly aware of the distaff except to be grateful for the convenience and pleasure it provides.

Bracelet-style wrist distaffs

This style of distaff is good for holding commercially prepared top or sliver of any fiber, for wool top you've combed yourself, or for sliver that you've prepared by pulling lengthwise on a drum-carded batt. To load the distaff, simply wind the fiber around its tail.

These distaffs are favored by spinners who like to have the fiber pass under the hand and who draft with their thumb and index finger. If you prefer to have the fiber come over your hand, these distaffs can be inconvenient because they tend to swing out and catch on the yarn.

My variations on this style of distaff are simpler yet. Instead of constructing the distaff by using macramé or braiding, you simply twist the yarn into position and use wrapping to hold it in place.

Four bracelet distaffs. These are all skein distaffs. The three on the left are twisted skein distaffs (hemp, silk, and kid mohair), and the one on the right is a two-skein twisted distaff (cotton bracelet and wool tail).

Twisted skein distaff

Materials and supplies

- Fiber of your choice. It can be anything that feels comfortable next to your skin. You'll need about ¼ ounce (7 g).

- A niddy noddy, skein winder, picture frame, box, or other object that measures about 48 inches (120 cm) in circumference. You'll wind the skein around this.

- Two loose-leaf binder rings from an office-supply store.

- Yarn needle.

- Scissors.

Instructions

1. Spin about 20 to 30 yards (18 to 27 m) of singles or overtwisted plied yarn. Singles or plied, use enough twist that the yarn feels lively and tries to double back on itself. The final thickness should be between 20 and 30 wraps per inch (2.5 cm).

Immediately make a skein that's about 48 inches (120 cm) in circumference by winding it around a niddy noddy, picture frame, or whatever. Leave the skein on the form while you tie together the two ends of the yarn and trim the tails off the knot.

2. Insert the binder rings at opposite ends of the skein, slide the skein off the form, and hold the rings to keep the skein stretched out as you carefully let the skein twist around itself. Now you have a twisted skein that's 24 inches (60 cm) long.

3. Fold the skein in half. Use some extra yarn (the same or contrasting) to make a snug wrapping at about the middle of the folded skein. Make sure the loop in the skein is big enough that you can comfortably slide it over your hand. Use the yarn needle to secure the tail ends of the wrapping yarn inside the wrapping, then trim the tails.

Option: Instead of wrapping, you can slide two tight-fitting beads onto the skein. These beads should be lightweight, with holes about ¼ inch (6 mm) in diameter.

4. Have someone hold the looped end or hook it over a knob to provide some tension. Take the two ends of the skein, which still have the rings in them, holding one in each hand. Untwist the ends enough to straighten them out, then continue twisting in the same direction until they have plenty of extra twist.

5. Let the ends twist around each other, guiding them so the result is nice and neat. This makes a twisted tail that hangs down from the bracelet. Use extra yarn to make a wrapping about 1 inch (2.5 cm) from the end of the tail, and use the yarn needle to secure the ends of the wrapping yarn. Then remove the rings and tease all the little loops apart to make a tassel.

To use a skein distaff, wrap prepared fiber around the hanging cord.

Two-skein twisted distaff

Materials and supplies

- Fiber of your choice. For this distaff it's fun to combine two different yarns, of the same or different colors. Try using a softer fiber for the bracelet part that fits on your wrist, and a coarser fiber for the tail part that you wrap the roving around.

- A niddy noddy, skein winder, picture frame, box, or any other object that measures about 24 inches (60 cm) in circumference. You'll wind the skeins around this.

- Two loose-leaf binder rings from an office-supply store.

- Scissors.

Instructions

1. For the bracelet part, spin about 10 to 15 yards (9 to 14 m) of singles or overtwisted plied yarn. Singles or plied, use enough twist that the yarn feels lively and tries to double back on itself. The final thickness should be about 20 to 30 wraps per inch (2.5 cm).

Immediately make this yarn into a skein about 24 inches (60 cm) in circumference. Tie the two yarn ends together and trim off the tails. Insert two binder rings at opposite positions, slide the skein off whatever you wrapped it around, and hold the rings to keep it stretched out as you carefully let it twist around itself. Now you have a twisted skein that's 12 inches (30 cm) long. Leave the rings in the ends.

2. For the tail part, spin another 10 to 15 yards (9 to 14 m) of yarn and make it into a skein 24 inches (60 cm) in circumference. Tie two loops of contrasting yarn in the skein and use them to keep the skein stretched out as you let it twist around itself.

3. This step is tricky. Fold the bracelet skein in half so the rings are side by side. Remove the rings and pass the tail skein through the two ends of the bracelet skein. Fold the tail skein in half, tug on it, and make any adjustments so that everything looks neat.

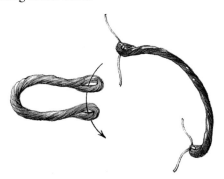

4. Now have someone hold the bracelet or hook it over an object to provide tension. Take the two ends of the tail skein, which have the contrasting yarn ties, and with one in each hand, untwist them enough to straighten them out. Keep twisting in the same direction to give them some extra twist.

5. Then let the two ends of the tail skein twist around each other, guiding them so the result is nice and neat. This makes a tail that hangs down from the bracelet. Make a snug yarn wrapping about 1 inch (2.5 cm) from the end of the tail or put a bead there. Remove the contrasting ties, and then tease the looped yarn ends apart to make a tassel.

Supertwist skein distaff

This simple project takes advantage of the elasticity of high-twist singles yarn. It's fast and easy to make, fun to use, and provides a great conversation piece at guild meetings or demonstrations. Basically, it's a small, lively skein that you can easily slide on and off of your wrist.

To load this distaff, attenuate a length of roving, top, or other fiber, then coil or fold it and insert it between the strands. The liveliness of the yarn holds the fiber in place and keeps it out of your way as you spin, but you can easily pull out more fiber when you need it. You can rotate the cuff so the fiber comes over or under your hand, whichever you prefer.

Materials and supplies
- Fiber of your choice. You'll need less than ¼ ounce (7 g). Making this distaff is a good way to see how different types of fiber react differently when twisted. Yarns spun from varying breeds of wool or kinds of cotton, from llama or alpaca, from mohair or other fibers can "absorb" more or less twist before they turn kinky, and it's interesting to experiment with that. For your first try, I recommend medium-fine wool or cotton. Both work well and feel soft next to your skin.

- A miniature niddy noddy, hardbound book, picture frame, or other object that measures about 18 inches (45 cm) in circumference. You'll wind the skein around this.

- Two pieces of yarn in a color that contrasts with your fiber, each 12 inches (30 cm) long.

- Yarn needle.

- Scissors.

Instructions
1. Spin a smooth, even singles that measures about 25 to 30 wraps per inch (2.5 cm). Use enough twist that the yarn kinks dramatically when you let it relax. This means a lot more twist than you would use for everyday purposes. To insert this much extra twist, you'll need to treadle many times more than you normally would before you let each length of yarn wind on.

If you find it hard to make a high-twist yarn on a single pass, try respinning instead. This is a traditional technique for making high-twist yarns. Spin as you normally would, then put the bobbin on your lazy kate, tie one end of the yarn onto the leader of a new bobbin, and respin the same yarn (turning the wheel in the same direction) to put more twist into it. You can respin the same yarn two, three, or more times until it has enough twist to be kinky.

2. After spinning, immediately wind the yarn into a skein by wrapping it around the object you selected. Keep the yarn under tension at all times as you wind the skein. Tie the two yarn ends together, making a tight knot.

3. Use two short pieces of a contrasting yarn to wrap very firmly around the skein in two places—where the ends are tied together and at the opposite side. Tie the ends of the wrapping yarns and trim off all tails. The wrappings keep the skein from getting tangled and provide places to grip when you slide the distaff on and off your wrist.

4. Remove the skein from whatever you wrapped it around. It will immediately collapse into a springy cuff. Put the cuff on your wrist.

5. To use this distaff, attenuate a length of fiber, coil or fold it, and insert it between the strands. The liveliness of the yarn will hold the fiber in place.

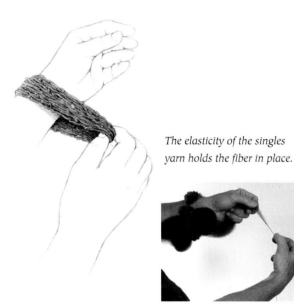

The elasticity of the singles yarn holds the fiber in place.

Knitted-cuff wrist distaffs

Before I started making and using distaffs, I liked to spin while wearing a long-sleeved sweatshirt or sweater, so I could tuck the fiber into the cuff of the garment. That worked fine from fall to spring, but who wears long sleeves in summer? It occurred to me that all I need is the cuff, not the sleeve, so I started making cuff distaffs. Now I use them year-round.

Circular-knitted

A knitted-cuff distaff should fit a bit more loosely than the cuff of a sweater or glove, and it can have a special feature—a compartment to hold the fiber. To load a

cuff distaff, tuck part of a drum-carded batt, some hand-carded rolags, or a length of pulled-out roving or top into the fiber compartment. Rotate the cuff so the fiber comes over or under your hand, whichever you prefer.

There are three ways to knit a cuff distaff. You can (1) work in the round, as you would make a glove cuff, and add the fiber compartment afterwards. If you make the cuff and compartment in a continuous strip by working back and forth on two needles, you can make either (2) a long, skinny strip or (3) a short, wide one. All three methods are described.

Materials and supplies

- About 20 to 30 yards (18 to 27 m) of yarn that measures about 15 to 20 wraps per inch (2.5 cm). The yarn can be singles or plied, made from any fiber that feels comfortable next to your skin. It's fun to use multicolored yarns for these distaffs.

- Knitting needles that are relatively small for the size of yarn you are using, to make a firm ribbed fabric.

Instructions

To make a **circular-knitted cuff**, figure a gauge based on your yarn and needle size. Loosely cast on enough stitches to make a cuff about 8 inches (20 cm) around. The number of stitches should be an even multiple of the ribbing pattern you will use (divisible by four for k2, p2 ribbing).

Using double-pointed needles, work the ribbing of your choice for about 2 inches (5 cm). Bind off loosely; check as you go to make sure the bound-off edge won't be too tight for you to slide the cuff on and off easily.

Now add the fiber compartment. Using the same or different yarn,

Long, skinny strip on two needles

pick up stitches along one rib, skipping every third or fourth stitch as you go. For example, if you worked 16 rows of ribbing, pick up about 12 stitches. Work back and forth on two needles in a mock ribbing or any stitch you choose.[1] For mock ribbing, I work *knit one row, purl one row, knit one row*; repeat from * to *. Continue until you have a flap about 4 inches (10 cm) long, then bind off.

Slide the cuff on your wrist, set some fiber on top, and fold the flap over the fiber to decide where to sew down the flap. Use a safety pin to hold the flap in place while you take the cuff off, then use the tail end of the yarn to stitch the end of the flap against a rib.

To knit a **long, skinny strip** on two needles, figure your gauge, then cast on enough stitches to make a piece about 2 inches (5 cm) wide.

Work back and forth on two needles in a mock ribbing (*knit one row, purl one row, knit one row*; repeat from * to *). When the piece is about 8 inches (20 cm) long, hold the ends together and try sliding the fabric over your hand. If you need to adjust the fit, add or rip out a few rows.

Then continue knitting in the same way, or change to a different yarn and/or stitch if you choose, and knit another 4 inches (10 cm) for the

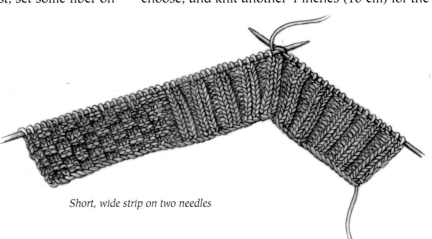

Short, wide strip on two needles

[1]What I call mock ribbing is just a type of horizontal ridges or welts. The idea is to simulate the look and elasticity of true ribbing. You can use a four-row repeat: *knit 2 rows, purl 2 rows*. That makes narrower welts, but it's much harder to keep track of what row you're on as you work than the three-row (knit-purl-knit) repeat.

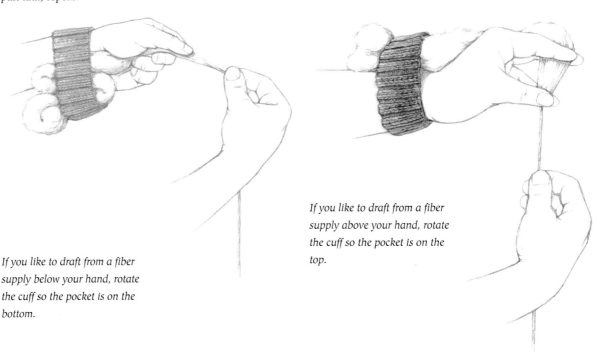

If you like to draft from a fiber supply below your hand, rotate the cuff so the pocket is on the bottom.

If you like to draft from a fiber supply above your hand, rotate the cuff so the pocket is on the top.

compartment. Bind off. Check the fit, baste the ends with safety pins, then sew them in place.

To knit a **short, wide strip on two needles,** figure your gauge, then cast on enough stitches to make a piece about 12 inches (30 cm) wide; use a number of stitches divisible by four.

Of the 12-inch (30-cm) width, work 8 inches (20 cm) for the cuff in k2, p2 ribbing and 4 inches (10 cm) for the compartment in whatever stitch you prefer. Work back and forth until the cuff is about 2 inches (5 cm) long, then bind off loosely.

Wrap the strip of knitting around your wrist, overlap the ends, and baste the fabric together with safety pins. Try sliding the cuff on and off a few times, stuff some fiber in the compartment, and adjust the overlap until it fits comfortably. Then sew the seams.

Stick distaffs

I've made dozens of these distaffs, using sticks from maple, ash, pine, viburnum, lilac, and other kinds of trees and shrubs, as well as dried flower stalks from angelica, wild parsnip, sunflower, and other stiff-stemmed garden plants and weeds. Once you start looking for stems with suitable branch patterns, you'll spot them all around your yard and neighborhood. Use pruning shears to harvest a likely distaff, cut it approximately to length, trim off any leaves or side shoots, then peel off the bark if you want to. Let the stick or stem dry for a week or two. Then you can sand it smooth with fine sandpaper, try it out, trim it to the final length, and apply a coat of oil if you like.

You can make stick distaffs in different styles and lengths. Lengths between 8 and 12 inches (20 and 30 cm) are suitable for hand-held stick distaffs. If you make a distaff between 30 and 36 inches (75 and 90 cm) long, you can support the bottom end in your waistband. This is very comfortable for sustained spinning at home, but long stick distaffs are awkward to take along when you're on the go.

The style, and how you attach the fiber, depends on whether the stick is straight or is forked, with two or more prongs.

To hold flicked locks of long-staple wool or a strick of flax, use a straight, unbranched stick. Lay the stick on a table, align one end of the fibers with the top end of the stick, and use a rib-

bon, string, or rubber band to secure the fibers to the stick. Draft by pulling down on the bottom ends of the fibers. You'll have to retighten the ribbon or other fastening device from time to time.

For top or roving, a forked stick with two prongs makes a good distaff, especially if you like to have the fiber coming down through your hand. Wind the roving in a figure-eight around the prongs. As you spin, you'll need to reach up from time to time and unwind another loop from the figure-eight.

For holding a batt of carded wool, a stick that branches into three, four, or more shoots is good.

All of these sticks will make good hand-held distaffs. Find a smooth stick you like and trim it to length—between 8 and 12 inches (20 and 30 cm) for a distaff that travels well.

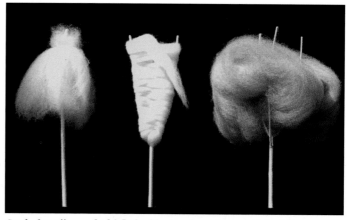

Stick distaffs can hold flicked locks of wool or a strick of flax (straight stick on left), prepared roving or top (two-pronged stick in center), or carded rolags or batts (three-pronged stick on right).

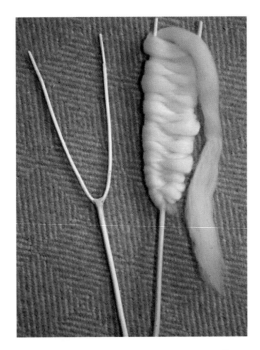

Wrap top or roving around a two-pronged stick with a figure-eight motion. You'll be surprised how much a small stick can hold.

Here's how to hold a stick distaff while you draft from it.

If the batt is small, simply spear the distaff through it and push the fiber down onto the prongs. If you have a large batt, fold or loosely roll it into a more compact shape before you spear it onto the distaff. When spinning, draft out fibers from any side of the batt and rotate the distaff from time to time, so you don't end up with a lopsided remainder.

Rita Buchanan is the associate editor of Spin·Off. *Although she's well-known within the spinning community for her thoughtful approach to the craft and her ability to teach so folks remember what they learned, spinners may not realize that Rita is also a gardener and garden writer. The combination of her interests led to her first book, A Weaver's Garden. For an introduction to more of Rita's work, we'd suggest that neophyte plant workers start with* Making a Garden: Reliable Techniques, Outstanding Plants, and Honest Advice *(Boston: Houghton Mifflin, 1998). More experienced green thumbs may want to head for* Taylor's Master Guide to Gardening *(Boston: Houghton Mifflin, 1994) or the* Home Landscaping Series, *divided into regional volumes (Upper Saddle River, New Jersey: Creative Homeowner Press, 1998, 1999). Rita and her husband, Steve Buchanan, also collaborate on regular features for in* Country Living Gardener.

Photo credit: Rita Buchanan

Resources

Crowfoot, Grace M. *Methods of Handspinning in Egypt and the Sudan.* Halifax, England: Bankfield Museum Notes, 1931. Reprinted in 1974 by Robin and Russ Handweavers, McMinnville, OR 97128.

Emerick, Patricia. "Wrist Distaffs." *Spin·Off* 19, no. 1 (Spring 1995): 70–73.

Hochberg, Bette. *Handspindles.* Revised edition. Santa Cruz, California: Bette and Bernard Hochberg, 1980. Published by Bette and Bernard Hochberg, 333 Wilkes Circle, Santa Cruz, CA 95060.

Quinn, Celia. "Spinning on a Takli Spindle." *Spin·Off* 19, no. 1 (Spring 1995): 82–84.

Winter 1999

Chapter Five

SPINNING AROUND THE WORLD

To survive, humankind has three needs: food, clothing, and shelter. Once these needs are met, everything else are desires. In primitive temperate cultures, these needs could be met with found materials. In harsh climates, hunter societies could meet all needs with food from the animal carcass, clothing and shelter from the hide. This was life at the barest sustenance level. As civilizations advanced, their needs became separate entities, each fulfilled in separate ways.

Weaving became the desirable way to clothe people. But weaving with found materials that required no further preparation was limited. People needed to spin to weave cloth on a large scale. As populations grew, spinning became one of the most historically significant aspects of world civilization. Although the end product was yarn, the method of achieving it varied widely from culture to culture. Yet all methods are irrevocably interrelated.

Today, handspinning no longer fulfills a need; industrialization of the textile industry provides abundant manufactured cloth. Today, we choose to spin; pursuing the craft has become a desire. But what we learn from our past and that of other cultures can significantly enhance the way that we, as spinners by choice, pursue our craft. It behooves us to learn as much we can from spinning around the world.

The High-Whorl Lap Spindle

Louise Heite

One of the must-see stops on any visit to Iceland is the Icelandic Handicraft Center in Reykjavik. All the handworks practiced in Iceland today are sold in their showroom, and in the winter they offer classes in Iceland's traditional crafts. While browsing through a rack of carved wooden items, I came upon a spindle with a hook in the "wrong" end.

Somewhat surprised, I took the spindle to the counter and asked the lady there about the unusual configuration. The clerk summoned another lady, apparently a spinner, who was about to go home. With some patience on all parts we overcame the language barrier and she showed me how to use the Icelandic high-whorl lap spindle.

Like the Icelandic sheep, this spindle is another survival from Viking times. Isolated and wracked with poverty, Icelanders maintained the customs, practices, and language of their ancestors long after those had evolved or disappeared from the rest of Scandinavia. Thus, although spinning wheels were not uncommon in 19th century Iceland, the lap spindle was neither abandoned nor forgotten even in this century.

The Icelandic lap spindle is used in a similar manner to the Navajo spindle, except that the whorl is towards the wool supply, and the cop of spun yarn is wound around the far end of the spindle shaft.

The first step in using the spindle is to prepare a long roving. The spindle is used only to insert twist, not to draft the yarn. Drafting is done as the roving is prepared. Once you've made the roving, insert the spindle hook into the end of the roving and twist it between your fingers. When you've spun a sufficient length of yarn, wrap it around the spindle shaft, back up over the whorl and through the hook. After the yarn is securely fastened to the spindle shaft, you can roll the spindle along your leg from hip to knee for faster spinning. With practice, it is possible to give the spindle enough of a spin that you can bring it back for its next push while it is still turning.

It may be necessary to twirl the spindle in your fingers several times until enough of a cop has built up to balance the weight of the whorl as the spindle rolls along your leg. Also, be careful to wind the yarn onto the shaft in the same direction as the spin, or it will unwind during the rolling motion.

The advantage of this kind of spinning is that it can be used to make extremely soft yarn. Because drafting and twisting are separate steps and the spindle is supported throughout the process, there is no strain on the yarn. You can use only the minimum twist necessary to hold the fibers together. This seems to be the secret to the traditionally soft and fluffy Icelandic knitting yarns.

The high-whorl lap spindle in use.

Spring 1986

The Spinners' Story

behind Russia's renowned shawls:
The goats and the spinning of Orenburg

Galina A. Khmeleva and Carol R. Noble

The goats and the fiber

Orenburg goats come from the steppes near the southern tip of the Ural Mountains. In Russia, their fleece is referred to as Orenburg down. The two most common colors are white and gray.

There is a legend from long ago that one goat lived eleven years. As he got older, his coat got lighter and lighter in color and finer and finer in texture. But this is just legend; goats live for five to six years. The best down comes from healthy goats who stay outside all winter—the long bitter cold weather on the steppes allows the down to grow long and full.

There are rare variations of color in down from the Orenburg region, such as silver and brown, that are of superior fiber quality and highly prized. These colors occur as a natural variation and produce fiber of a very fine micron count. Some think that brown may have been the original color of the goats early in the development of the breed. At the turn of the century, a Russian historian named Davidova reported on the popularity of the thick brown warm shawls—warm as fur coats and of very high quality—that were shipped to Siberia but also available in department stores in St. Petersburg and Moscow. But by the 1960s and 1970s, brown shawls fell out of favor with Russian women; they were thought of as a *babushka* peasant color, and efforts were made to breed the more fashionable goats of silver, white, and dark gray. The result of this misguided breeding is the extreme rarity of brown goats today. Breeding efforts aimed at "improving" the down and meat and increasing production per animal have resulted in longer, harsher, and straighter fiber. Efforts are now under way to back-breed to the original brown.

The goats are combed in February/ March and again twenty to twenty-five days later. Goat combs have a wooden handle and six to eight steel hooks. The fiber is preferably not cut from the goats because cut fiber sheds when knitted up. First-quality combed down has less than 10 per-

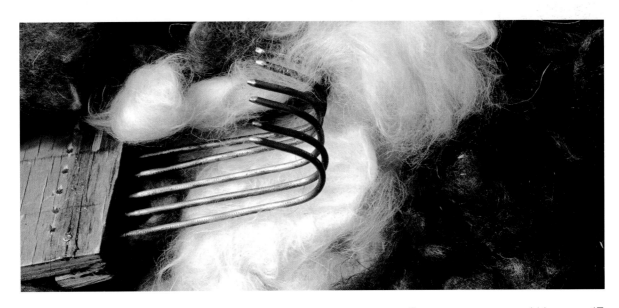

Down from the Orenburg region naturally varies in color.

Spindles range from ten to fifteen inches (25.5 to 38 cm) in length and are less than one inch (2.5 cm) in diameter.

The best down comes from healthy goats who stay outside all winter.

cent guard hair; second-quality has 10 to 20 percent guard hair. Down with more than 20 percent guard hair is considered third quality, and is used to make lower quality products such as socks, mittens, scarves, and hats. In Moslem Tatar families, the mother-in-law knits her prospective son-in-law down socks which he will wear throughout his marriage whenever he comes to visit her. If the socks last a long time, it is said he doesn't visit his mother-in-law often enough.

Although by tradition yarn has been produced by hand, it should be pointed out that many, perhaps the majority, of the shawls produced during the later days of the Kombinat[1] were knitted from white machine-spun yarn that was hand-plied with silk. This machine-spun yarn is produced mostly on collective farms in the Orenburg region. It contains considerable guard hair which must be picked out. Some knitters ply with viscose, which is cheap and makes a crinkly, shiny shawl. Since the collapse of the Kombinat, there has been an effort to foster the use of handspun yarn. For warm shawls, which are always gray now, the down is spun heavier and then plied with three strands of dark brown or dark gray cotton. The process is otherwise the same, although the yarn produced is thicker and stronger, and the shawls heavier and warmer.

Spinning

Before spinning, raw Orenburg down must be cleaned to remove dirt and debris while leaving in the natural oils. To wash, soak down in 104° to 122°F (40° to 50°C) water with a small amount of clear or white liquid dish soap. Do not squeeze or agitate the down. Rinse to remove the soap and hang the washed and rinsed down on a clothesline to partially dry. When it is almost dry, roll it up in a damp cloth.

The next step is to remove the guard hairs. Tease the down by handfuls into fiber "clouds." Tease the fibers parallel and, working over a white

---

[1] *The Kombinat was a cottage industry that evolved out of the Orenburg Down Center, established in 1938. For almost thirty years, the Kombinat supplied tools and materials to knitters, set standards for production, and marketed finished shawls. But the Kombinat folded at the end of 1995, setting knitters adrift in the difficult economic climate of present-day Russia.*

Center a handful of down over the comb, then lower it onto the teeth.

Gently pull hands apart.

You will now have two sections of down.

Put the two sections of down one on top of the other and repeat the process six to seven times.

cloth for gray down or a dark cloth for white down, pull out all the long guard hairs. Be sure to remove every hair.

Combing is the next step. In Orenburg, combing is done on a triangular wooden frame with closely spaced metal teeth about two inches (5 cm) high in a double row along the top edge. The frame is anchored with a bent knee or a thigh. This type of frame probably came to Orenburg

Forming a Rolag

To make a small rolag, overlap the tips and ends of fibers, aligning them parallel to each other.

Roll the fibers up from the bottom.

Fibers are now perpendicular to the length of the rolag.

along the silk road from Central Asia where it was used by carpet makers.

Small handfuls of down are easiest to comb. In Orenburg, spinners say it takes twenty years' experience to be able to comb large handfuls easily and quickly. Pick up a handful of down, one end in each hand, and center it over the comb, then lower it onto the teeth and pull the hands apart. You will have two sections of down—one in each hand. Put these one on top of the other and repeat the process six to seven times with each handful. This first combing breaks knots and clears debris.

The second combing, a repeat of the whole process, serves to align the fibers. While combing, periodically work any knotted fiber out of the teeth and throw it away. Pull out the short fibers and save them for socks and mittens.

When you have approximately 3.5 ounces (100 g) of combed down, divide the pieces into five even piles. Form each pile into a rolag—a tube of fleece in which the fibers are perpendicular to the direction of spinning. To make a rolag, begin by laying out a line of combed down about one yard (one meter) long, overlapping the tips and ends and aligning the fibers parallel to each other. Roll the fiber up from the bottom—the fibers now go around the "tube" and are perpendicular to the length of the rolag. Each rolag will become one spindle of spun yarn, and it takes between five and six spindles to make a shawl.

If you are working with gray fleece, there is one additional step in the process. The down from different parts of a gray goat varies in color, so you should card the combed gray fleece to blend the colors before forming it into rolags.

Orenburg spinners use a different spindle for each rolag. The wooden spindles, hand lathed or hand carved, are made of a lightweight wood. Their shape is particular to the region—the spindles are made in one piece and include a tiny low whorl with tapering ends and a fat body. Spindles range from ten to fifteen inches (25.5 to 38 cm) in length and are less than one inch (2.5 cm) in diameter. The whorl and spindle circumferences are usually about the same. The shorter, more delicate spindles are used for spinning and the larger versions for plying.

The spindle is supported in a small bowl, and spinning is done over a dark cloth. To begin, separate out a handful of rolag, pull out a few fibers from the end of the "tube," and while holding the upper tip of the spindle, spin these fibers around the tip clockwise. When you have spun six to eight inches (15 to 20.5 cm) this way, take the yarn off the top and wrap it around the fat part of the spindle, above the neck that connects the whorl. Hold the top of the spindle cupped in the fingertips of one hand and twirl it to put twist into the fiber. In the other hand, hold the rolag between your thumb and index finger and use the middle finger to draft the fibers in a fan.

There are three motions going on at the same time: spinning, drafting, and pulling out. The spindle should be held vertically. A moderate overtwist at this point is desirable. Starting at the base, wind the thread onto the spindle in a circle one inch (2.5 cm) wide. When this section is comfortably full, move up and make a new circle one inch (2.5 cm) wide. It takes a proficient Russian spinner approximately five hours to spin one-half ounce (15 g) of clean down onto one spindle, five to six days to spin enough yarn for a gossamer shawl measuring 63 by 63 inches (160 by 160 cm) and weighing 3 ounces (90 g). The yarn is stored on the spindle until plying.

The next stage in yarn production is plying. To create the traditional Orenburg blend of down and silk, use a larger plying spindle, one strand of fine silk (Orenburg spinners use silk that is commercially spun in Uzbekistan and has the consistency of fine sewing thread), and one strand of your handspun. Roll the two threads counterclockwise onto the spindle. Hold the two threads together between the thumb and index finger, and with these fingers touching the spindle to apply a little tension, use the other hand to twist the spindle, winding the double strand onto it the same way you did when spinning.

The next step is like spinning in reverse. When the plying spindle is full, pull out a length of yarn with one hand and twist the tip of the spindle with the other. This puts twist into the pulled-out yarn. Wrap the twisted yarn around a cardboard bobbin approximately two inches (5 cm) in diameter. The motion is pull out, twist, and wrap. As you continue to ply, wind the plied yarn onto the bobbin until it is full. It will take numerous bobbins to hold all the plied yarn which should have 180 twists per 39 inches (100 cm).

Spinning

Spin fibers in a clockwise direction.

When you have spun six to eight inches (15 to 20.5 cm), wrap the yarn around the fat part of the spindle.

Hold the top of the spindle with the fingertips of one hand and twirl it to put twist into the fiber.

The spindle should be held vertically.

Wind the thread onto the spindle in a circle one inch (2.5 cm) wide.

When finished, wrap full bobbins in a wet cloth and keep them in a warm place until the cloth is dry. This will set the twist.

Galina Alexandrovna Khmeleva is a native Russian who, as a young woman, was drawn to Orenburg by the mystique of the region's cobweb lace. There we learned both the art form and its history. Galina teaches workshops on Orenburg lace-knitting techniques throughout the United States.

Carol Rasmussen Noble has been an avid textile collector for thirty years. She is a professional knitter and writer who has done extensive traveling, including a one-month stay in Orenburg while doing research for Gossamer Webs.

This article is excerpted from Gossamer Webs, *a book from Interweave Press which chronicles the evolution of Orenburg lace shawls (November 1998, $21.95). Written from both historical and technical perspectives, the book introduces eight of the region's most prolific shawl artists and provides information which will help readers make shawls of their own.* The Gossamer Webs Design Collection *is now available from Interweave Press, $12.95, 800-289-9276.*

Winter 1998

Plying

To ply, roll the two threads counter-clockwise onto the spindle.

Wrap the plied yarns onto bobbins.

To wrap bobbins, the motion is pull out, twist, and wrap.

Wind yarn onto the bobbin until it is full.

Andean Spinning...

slower by the hour, faster by the week

Ed Franquemont

The variety of procedures and equipment used around the world to accomplish a basic task like making yarn is truly astonishing. The Andean area alone has been home to many different systems of spinning, about which relatively little is known. Cotton spinners of the lowland Amazonian basin work their fiber with supported spindles and small whorls, while a recently recognized group of cotton spinners from the North coast of Peru make yarn on spindles held horizontally and worked like a great wheel. Wool spinners from the high mountains show similar diversity of technique. In parts of Ecuador, wool is worked with horizontal spindles like those of north coastal Peru, while in Huancavelica, a vertical spindle with a removable whorl is employed with a curious and clumsy Y-shaped distaff.

This article will focus on a third system for spinning wool that is in wide use throughout most of the Peruvian and Bolivian sierra. The spindle (called *pushka* in Quechua) has a relatively narrow diameter and tapers toward the top; a disc-shaped whorl (Quechua: *tillu*) is dropped onto the spindle from above and therefore cannot be removed during spinning. There is seldom any visual decoration on the whorl, but occasionally lathe-turned whorls will have a captive ring that rattles as the spindle turns—an audio decoration, if you will; called a *chak-chak* spindle. Spinners of the Cuzco area never use a distaff, but wrap the prepared roving around their wrists to keep it out of trouble. Usually a larger, heavier spindle of the same kind (Q.: *kanti*) is used for plying.

Although occasionally people may clip a section of a living fleece, most Cuzco-area handspinners take their best fleece from the hides of slaughtered sheep whose fleece has been growing for several years. Shearing is discouraged by the consistently cold temperatures at high altitudes which put a freshly shorn animal at risk. The fleece is prepared simply with the fingers (Q.: *unchay*, to make small) by spreading and cleaning the fiber to an even density and then pulling it out along the axis of the fiber into a rough roving. Since the spinning continues to draw in the same direction, this is a worsted spinning system. Cleaning and preparing the fleece is busy work that is frequently given to children to keep them out of mother's way or in idle moments visiting each others' houses. But, in fact, we have seen many people spinning directly from the fleece with little or no preparation at all.

The motions of Cuzco spinning are extremely efficient, but to call them "drop spindle spinning" is a serious confusion. In fact, spinning this way is a two part process: first, 1) yarn formation, which uses a controlled and not dropped spindle; and then 2) surface finishing, which imparts twist and allows the yarn to feel the weight of the spindle. In addition, there are several hand and finger tricks that are crucial to the system: a) figure-8 storage on the fingers, b) dropping half hitches onto the spindle shaft with one hand, and c) doubling a single thread to find the two ends. We have found written instructions such as these to be barely useful, if at all, in learning this spinning system, for most of these tricks must be seen to be understood and then practiced. About 12 hours of practice will teach almost anyone to be a passable spinner with the Cuzco system.

Yarn formation

Hold the spindle lightly in your right hand and slowly turn it to impart twist without dropping the spindle. Draw the fleece out with the left hand so that the small amount of twist collects in the thin places. Continue to turn and tug so that the draw pulls the thicker,

Ed Franquemont

unspun sections out until the twist from the thin places begins to creep out and spreads itself more evenly throughout the yarn. Use the spin twist to indicate evenness, and continue to turn gently and tug until a relatively uniform yarn size has been achieved in a length of yarn nearly the distance between your outstretched arms.

Wind the formed but only lightly twisted yarn on the fingers of your left hand with a cross in a figure-8 pattern. Any combination of fingers will do, but the first two fingers are usually the most graceful. The winding keeps the yarn out of trouble while it is slack.

Surface finishing

Spin the spindle fairly strongly with your right hand and let it fall. Feed the formed yarn out of the figure-8 storage on your left hand and run it through the thumb and middle finger of the left hand. As you find thick places with your left hand, pinch the yarn below the thickening with your right hand, back spin slightly and draw it out to the proper diameter. Be sure to run all yarn through the thumb and middle finger to tuck in the loose ends. Continue and repeat until the

desired amount of spin has entered the entire length of yarn.

a) Re-wind the finished yarn with the figure-8 and cross onto the fingers of the left hand.

b) Slip the knots (Q.: *senq'opaj*) off the end of the spindle and wind the finished yarn onto the spindle shaft near the whorl. Form half hitches around the thumb of the right hand and drop them onto the spindle shaft.

Chinchero spinners working with this system have averaged nearly 1.5 meters of yarn per minute of work in producing their standard Z-spun singles, with the best of them reaching nearly 2 meters per minute. Several claimed to handle nearly a kilo of yarn a day, but these studies show that it takes nearly 20 hours of work to spin a pound of yarn. Despite the availability of several spinning wheels in the town, people continue to prefer the handspindle methods. While mechanical advantage would improve the figures on ten-minute samples like those we made in our study of production rates, there are very real cultural and even production advantages in handspindle work. Spinning becomes a habit, a constant companion that draws the spinner into the rhythms of daily life in the Andes. It is no accident that our best spinners from Chinchero were full-time shepherds, whose lives are characterized by constancy. Production, like life itself, is a process and not a goal to be achieved; the bursts of occasional but intense and directed energy associated with wheel spinning do not fit well into this process. Habitual handspindle spinning meshed into a daily routine is indeed slower by the hour, but faster by the week.

Ed Franquemont studied Andean anthropology and archeology as Harvard University and has been conducting field studies for nearly twenty years. As an active handweaver, he was drawn to the spectacular fabrics of ancient Peru and ultimately into work with contemporary Quechua weavers. Ed regularly lectures and conducts workshops across the United States.

Spring 1985

Ed Franquemont

Benito Gutierrez G., left, is preparing fleece to spin onto the nearly full spindle in front of her. Nazariea Quispe Q., right, is spinning from prepared fleece wrapped around her wrist in the standard Cuzco-area method. Between her right hand and the spindle is finished yarn. She is in the yarn formation part of the process between her hands.

Spinning on a Navajo Spindle:

A Visit with Sarah Natani

Donna Muller

A Navajo spindle is a special type of supported spindle with a long wooden shaft and a large wooden whorl. The Navajos have traditionally used these spindles to change hand-carded wool and mohair into warp and weft yarns for their famous rugs, but you can also use a Navajo spindle for other fibers and other kinds of yarns. It's a versatile tool.

Navajo yarn is almost always spun twice. The first step, soft spinning, makes lightly twisted roving. Then this roving is spun a second time, drafting it down to the desired grist and adding considerably more twist. Soft spinning and "regular" spinning are both done with Z twist. Navajo three-ply yarn is made with S twist.

For a look at the traditional techniques, follow these photos of Sarah Natani, a spinner and weaver who lives near Shiprock, New Mexico. Sarah is one of the few Navajo weavers who continues to spin her own yarns, using fiber from her own flock of sheep and Angora goats. She has demonstrated and taught at Convergence, SOAR, and other fiber conferences around the United States, and was the featured Navajo weaver on a PBS program about rugs from all over the world.

The spindle

The right length for a Navajo spindle depends on your spinning position. It must reach from your thigh to the floor, so a shorter spindle is appropriate for sitting on the floor, while a longer one is used for spinning when seated in a chair. Sarah says the shorter ones are "old style, from when we didn't use so much furniture in our houses." Sarah's collection includes some special spindles, including an old one with a fragile bark whorl which is protected with piñon pine pitch, one inset with turquoise and coral, and two decorated with hand carving on the whorls. They range in length from about as long as her forearm to longer than her arm.

A good spindle must have an absolutely straight shaft. The size and weight of the whorl may vary, but about 4 to 4½ inches (10 to 11 cm) in diameter is "a good learning size." If the whorl is too heavy, "your hand will get tired," said Sarah, waggling her right thumb, which supports the spindle.

Getting started

With a Navajo spindle, you don't seem to have any hands left over for fussing with your fiber, so when you're learning, use medium-long,

Sarah's spindles come in different lengths—some are as long as her forearm, others longer than her entire arm. Those for use while sitting on the ground are shorter than those she uses for spinning at chair-height.

Soft-spun

To start spinning without a leader, poke the tip of the spindle through the end of a rolag, twist the rolag together a bit around the shaft, then poke the tip through the rolag again right next to the twisted part.

Slide the rolag down the shaft a few inches

Twirl the spindle and spiral the rolag several times around the spindle.

not-too-crimpy wool that drafts easily, and card it into loose fluffy rolags. There's a trick for getting started with just a rolag and a spindle. You don't just tie a piece of yarn onto the spindle and join onto it—that would be cheating. Instead, hold the spindle with the bottom tip (the whorl end) on the floor a few inches away from your thigh, on your right side. You'll use your right hand to spin the spindle, and the left hand to hold the fiber. Poke the tip of the spindle through the end of the rolag, twist the rolag as if you were fastening a twist-'em around the spindle shaft, then push the spindle tip through the rolag again, right next to the twisted part. Slide the rolag down the shaft about 8 inches (20 cm).

Soft spinning

For soft spinning, Sarah does not roll the spindle on her thigh, but twirls it between her fingers in a more upright position. She says the thigh is for "the real spinning." Soft spinning goes fast, putting in just enough twist to hold the wool together. The goal is to make a roving that will, in the next step, be drawn out to about three times its length.

Holding the spindle upright with your right hand, pinch the middle of the rolag with your left hand. Twirl the spindle between your thumb and first two fingers, rolling it back along your thumb. The twirl is back toward you. This makes a Z twist.

Slide the fuzzy wrapping off the tip of the spindle (keeping the twisted part from leaving the shaft) and draft out the slightly twisted fiber into a roving that's about the same length as the spindle shaft.

From this point, all spinning occurs off the tip of the shaft. Put in twist, then pull the rolag to draft it into roving.

As you twirl the spindle, the rolag will wind around the shaft. (You may have to secure the twisted-on end of the rolag as you begin to turn the spindle.) Rotate the spindle several times to spiral the rolag up to the tip. The rolag isn't twisted yet; it's just wrapped around the shaft. Now slide this fuzzy wrapping off the tip of the spindle, leaving just the end attached. There are as many twists in that portion of rolag as the number of wraps around the shaft. Pull on the rolag to draw it out into a piece of roving a little longer than the length of your spindle shaft from whorl to tip. Sarah makes this first half-rolag come out just long enough—about 18 inches (45 cm)—in one pass. You may have to twist and tug a second time to get it right. Push the roving down to the whorl with your right hand, keeping a little tension on it. Holding the spindle upright, twirl it in toward you (in the same direction as you twist the roving) so the roving winds around and up the shaft to the tip.

Now you're ready to soft-spin the second half of this rolag, and to continue with the rest of your rolags. From now on, all spinning occurs off the tip of the shaft. Holding it upright, twirl the spindle enough to put in about ten twists, then pull between your hands to draft the wool into a length of roving. Turn the spindle in the other direction to unwind the roving that's spiraling up the shaft (you'll have to extend your arms to do this), then turn back in the regular direction again to wind the roving around the base of the spindle just above the whorl, leaving enough to spiral back up to the tip of the shaft. When asked about winding the yarn on the spindle, Sarah said, "any way's okay as far as I can see," though she acknowledged that, "some of the older ladies are very particular."

To continue soft-spinning, repeat the same steps again and again. Twist-and-draft part of a rolag; unwind the roving that was on the shaft and wind it near the whorl; wind the next length of roving up the shaft; and begin the twist-and-draft again. Proceed with half a rolag at a time. To join on more wool, overlap a little of the new rolag on top of the previous one. Sarah folds the rolag lengthwise at the join and gives it a little half-twist to secure it.

Here's the drafting of that same length, continued.

Unwind the roving that's spiraling up the shaft, then turn the regular direction to wind the roving around the spindle just above the whorl.

To join on the next rolag, overlap a little of the new rolag on top of the previous one.

When the spindle's full, Sarah starts a small ball, then pulls the yarn off in long loops and drops them on top of the ball. At the end, she flips the pile, finds the start of the ball, and winds the rest of the fiber onto it.

Here are some of Sarah's exotic spindles: left, inset with turquoise and coral; center, carved in Japan; right, an old-style spindle with a piñon pitch coating.

Yarn

Roll the spindle against your thigh, and move your opposite hand back along the roving to guide in the twist.

Sarah doesn't hesitate to use both hands to get the roving even for the final spinning.

When the yarn is twisted enough, wind it onto the spindle.

Doffing the spindle

Eventually you have to take the roving off the spindle. How much is a spindleful? A lot. Sarah holds up a very soft ball the size of a basketball and says that is one spindleful. But making a ball like this is a two-step process unless you have an assistant, because unwinding roving off the spindle and working on a ball are both two-hand jobs.

Here's how Sarah does it alone. First she unwinds some roving off the spindle and wraps it five or six times around her hand to make a nice soft core, then wraps a few more times, until the ball is the size of a baseball. To "make it go faster," she puts the small ball down on the floor, with a cloth or apron underneath. Then she unwinds the roving off the spindle in long loops and drops them on top of the ball. Once the whole spindle is unwound into what looks like a hopeless loopy lump, she takes the pile, flips it over, and proceeds to wind the rest of the ball.[1] She says you may want to put a second cloth over the pile before flipping it, and you should certainly put the whole business between two cloths if you're going to leave it before getting it safely into a ball.

Once the ball is finished—very big and loose—you've come to the very beginning and, in Sarah's soft-spun, you can find the little loophole where the roving first went over the spindle. Poke that loop over the tip of the spindle (or make another one) and you're ready to start spinning yarn.

"Real spinning"— making yarn

Sarah says it's very important to start spinning your yarn from the end where you started your soft-spun. Otherwise, "it will get tangles and have a lot of lumps because it will be like spinning backwards." Spinning proceeds by putting

---

[1] I've also seen Sarah make a soft roving ball by extending her legs and catching both ends of the spindle shaft under her big toes, freeing both hands to wind as the shaft rolls behind her toes.

more twist into a small section of roving to make it stronger, drafting it out to the final thickness, then putting the desired amount of twist into that finalized length of roving, and winding it onto the spindle.

You can sit on the floor or in a chair. Sarah's favorite spinning stool is a little shorter than a chair and has a bigger seat, like a large ottoman. There's room to put her ball of roving on the upholstered surface next to her left hip.

You might want to practice twirling the spindle before you actually start to spin. Rest the spindle against your right thigh at about a 45° angle, with about 4 to 6 inches (10 to 15 cm) of the shaft above your thigh. With your right hand, rotate the spindle shaft against your thigh, rolling backward with your palm, then your fingers. The motion is like wiping your hand on your jeans, palm first, from your knee back toward your hip—but the spindle is underneath your hand, so the wiping motion twirls the spindle. When you've wiped all the way to your finger tips, you catch the spindle in the V at the base of your thumb and move it out near your knee again for another wiping roll backward.

When you're ready to spin, pinch off about 6 inches (15 cm) of roving. Twist the spindle between your fingers to put a little more twist into the roving, then draft the 6 inches (15 cm) out to about 18 inches (45 cm). Sarah doesn't hesitate to take her right hand off the spindle and use both hands to tug at the roving to get it even for the final spinning.

After drafting about 18 inches (45 cm) of roving, use your left hand to hold the roving near the tip of the spindle. (Let the rest of the roving lie on your lap.) Start twirling the spindle by rolling it against your thigh, and move your left hand back along the roving to guide in the twist. How much should you twist it? That depends on how you want to use the yarn. It takes several rolls to twist the roving into Sarah's "regular yarn," which is a densely twisted singles weft for rug weaving. Her warp yarn is even more tightly twisted, to give it strength and abrasion resistance. When you think that the yarn is twisted enough, wind it onto the spindle. Then pinch off another 6-inch (15-cm) length of roving and start again.

Making Navajo three-ply yarn

Before she demonstrated plying, Sarah said, "Okay, move everything out of the way," and started shoving her 50-pound (20-kilo) onion bag of fleece, several spindles, and a couple of soft-spun balls all well out of range. She emptied her apron pockets, too, really clearing the decks. Sarah does three-ply from another of those terrifying loopy piles. Holding the spindle upright on her lap, she unwinds the yarn with one hand and lets it drop onto the floor beside her. She doesn't make a ball but just starts plying from the top of the pile, which would be the outside of the ball, had she made one. She says it's good to put this pile between two cloths, too, just like the roving, if you're going to leave it. (I'd also put the cats out for the duration—and maybe anything else in the house that moves.) Sarah says, "We can't really explain why it doesn't get tangles . . . and it will get tangles sometimes. It's by the way you move it, I think, when you undo it." My best interpretive advice is to lay each series of loops carefully down on top of the last.

Switch to a smaller Navajo spindle for plying, if you have one, and stand it upright in your lap. Put that same little beginning loophole over the spindle and slide it about two-thirds of the way down the shaft toward the whorl. Make a loop over the top of the whorl and back again, so there's a squat Z of three strands of yarn about a foot long: from the spindle to your left hand, back to the spindle, and out to your hand again. Collapse the Z downward on the spindle with your right hand.

Now, this is the trick to Navajo plying. With your left hand, catch the free end of the yarn and pull a second loop through the first one. Then continue pulling one loop through another, like making a chain in crochet.

For twisting the chain of loops into a three-ply yarn, you

Before plying, Sarah unloops the singles into a pile on the floor.

Plying

Far left. Start to ply by making a loop over the top of the whorl and back again, so there's a Z of three strands of yarn about a foot (30 cm) long.

Middle and left. Collapse the loop downward on the spindle. Catch the free end of the yarn and pull a second loop through the first one. Continue this; it's like making a crocheted chain.

turn the spindle around, so the long part of the shaft points away from you, and spin off the tip of the short end. Hold all three strands taut with your left hand, flip the spindle over so it rests on your lap parallel to the floor, bring the yarn over the whorl to the short end of the shaft, and wrap the yarn around once or twice to secure it.

Then roll the spindle down your thigh, pushing it toward your knee. You're wiping fingertips-to-palm this time. Catch the spindle with your fingers crooked, to bring it back up your thigh for the next swipe. This is a trickier gesture than the roll and catch of regular spinning. It feels backward, and it is, because you're putting an S ply into the Z-spun yarn.

When you have as much twist as you want in the three-ply, unwind it from the short end of the spindle and wind it onto the long end of the shaft, next to the whorl. Then bring it back over the whorl and wrap it around the short end as before.

You can make loops as long as you can reach. Just be careful to pull on all three strands to straighten them out and get the tension even

before you twist the spindle to ply them together. Sarah has a clever way of making very long loops. As she draws the free end through a loop, she winds lots of yarn in a little bundle in her left hand. Then she gradually releases it, carefully pulling it out into a single loop 2 or 3 yards (2 or 3 meters) long. That means those little bumps at the ends of the loops are spaced far apart in her yarn, not that it really matters in the long run. As she says, you never notice the place where a loop was formed "unless you cut it there and see."

Making a skein

Sarah's last trick is to make a skein by wrapping yarn off the spindle onto one hand and one extended foot. She ties the skein with its own two ends and says that's all the security it needs. To set the twist, she washes the yarn and weights the skein while it dries.

Donna Muller divides her time between Massachusetts and Arizona, and takes on all interesting

Sarah reverses the position of the spindle for plying: she inserts twist off the tip of the short end of the shaft. Bring the yarn over the whorl and wrap it around the shaft to secure it.

Roll the spindle down your thigh, catch the spindle with your fingers crooked, and bring it back up your thigh for the next rotation.

tasks with enthusiasm. Perhaps best-known for her weaving expertise—she's the author of Handwoven Laces *(Loveland, Colorado: Interweave Press, 1991)—she has recently been showing up more often in spinning realms. We're glad to have her here!*

Spring 1995

When the three-ply is adequately twisted, unwind it from the short end of the spindle and wind it onto the long end, next to the whorl.

As long as the three strands are evenly tensioned, you can make the loops as long as you want. When she draws the free end through a loop to make the next loop, Sarah winds a bundle of yarn into her hand. As she slowly releases this off her fingertips, it makes a single loop 2 to 3 yards (2–3 m) long.

For skeining, yarn is unwrapped from the spindle around one hand and one extended foot.

Interested in a versatile spinning tool? The Navajo spindle rewards the time spent in mastering it. At the top right is soft-spun; the white is typically unwashed, and the rusty orange ball was dyed in the fleece, which is unusual.

The three-strand braided cord was made from Donna Muller's first Navajo-style spinning, Navajo-plied and made into an all-purpose rope. Sarah says that a girl's first spinning project is often a braid like this, which would typically be used in the construction of a loom and would spend many years in service.

The skeins were spun by Sarah's mother, Mary Lee Henderson, in what Sarah calls "the old way." The yarns are spun hard, to wear well in rugs. The yellow was dyed, most likely with rabbitbrush. The browns are natural colors, typical of a Two Grey Hills flock.

The spindle itself holds hand-dyed silk sliver, spun by Deborah Robson while visiting at the Maryland Sheep and Wool Festival.

Spinning with Susie

Ron Chacey

Visiting with people of various ethnic origins that are involved with handspinning and weaving wool, especially those that have black sheep, has been a desire of many handspinners. While traveling in the southwestern United States in the summer of 1982 for the purpose of seeing the desert country, this wish was somewhat fulfilled for me. I was not expecting to visit and spin with a Navajo Indian woman who keeps sheep of various colors.

Susie Yazzi of Monument Valley, Arizona, keeps some black sheep with her flock of white sheep. She cards, spins, and weaves the wool from her sheep, and she is able to show and share all of this with prearranged visitors. I should add that this is how she makes her living, and donations are expected. However, the donations are far less than the expense of getting there in the first place.

After a fantastic drive through Monument Valley, we arrived at Susie's camp. Within two minutes, five Angora goats had crawled under my truck. Only in the last couple of years has it become a permanent camp, making it easier to have visitors. My only disappointments were that the sheep were off grazing in another canyon far away, and that the two young women in the family that spoke English had gone to town that day. However, we were able to communicate some with Susie. When there was a lot of desire, there are always ways to communicate without spoken language.

Susie and her family live in a stucco block house, and we had a wonderful lunch with them under a shade tree nearby. During lunch, a guide brought some people to the camp, and Susie left us for a while to show them her spinning and weaving. After she'd finished, Susie let us to the hogan where she does her work, and we were given a demonstration of how she cards and spins. The yarn was then woven into the rug on which she was currently working. The rug was done in traditional Navajo style. The loom was vertical and suspended from a beam with ropes, and the weft was beaten in with a standard tapestry technique.

Before visiting with Susie, my knowledge of Navajo spinning was limited to information from articles that I had read over the years. I do not know if there are variations, or what they might be, in the techniques used by different Navajo spinners; the following information comes mostly from my experience with Susie. The analysis of yarn and wool qualities is my own. Due to lack of communication in English, there is information that I was not able to acquire with certainty.

Susie keeps a flock of sheep that is made up of many colors. She and her family graze their sheep in several of the remote canyons of the Monument Valley. The wool she uses is scoured and dyed before being spun. They shear and scour the wool from their own sheep, and they also buy some wool that has already been scoured and dyed. The white, gray, brown, and black colors are produced by using undyed wool from natural colored sheep. The cards and carding technique that Susie used were very similar to that used by most spinners.

Navajo spinning is done while seated on the ground. The spindle used is approximately 18" long and has the whorl placed about 6" up the shaft from the bottom end. It has many similarities to the common drop spindle; however, the technique of using the Navajo spindle is very different. The longer shaft and its extension beyond the whorl are very necessary in order to effective at spinning using the Navajo technique.

The spindle is rested on the ground with the upper end of the shaft against the thigh. One hand rolls the spindle against the thigh while the other hand holds the rolag of wool and drafts the yarn single-handed—during the first step, that is. The spinning is done in several stages. First a large, bulky yarn (not much different than a rolag) is spun for about 18" with a very, very light twist. Then, while not rolling the spindle, both hands are used to pull the bulky low-twist yarn (small sections at a time) out into a less bulky yarn that is approximately double the length. This is then given more twist, but still lightly. Once again, while not rolling the spindle, both hands are used to pull the yarn to almost the size that the finished yarn is to be. During all of this process none of the yarn has been rolled up onto the spindle.

While spinning the yarn for the third time, several actions are going on at once. The spindle is rolled most of the time. However, quite often the spindle is stopped and the yarn is pulled with both hands to even it out. The final twist put on the yarn is very tight. During the final spinning, as each 1½' to 2' are finished, that length is wound onto the spindle. The original 18" of soft, bulky yarn ends up being about 4' to 5' of finished yarn.

Ed. note: Although not well documented, this method of "double spinning" is not uncommon among the elderly Navajo spinner-weavers. These women, many illiterate, learned their techniques by observing the traditions of their mothers, aunts, and grandmothers. Double spinning, whereby the entire roving is prepared then re-spun into the final yarn, has been documented in numerous sources. The literate generations, many now in their fifties and sixties, appear to have been influenced by this documentation. P.G-R

While watching Susie spin, I couldn't help but think how similar it was, in total effect, to double drafting (unsupported long draw). This was helpful in understanding the process, but it also indicated the biggest problem that I was to have in trying to learn the technique. I am accustomed to finishing yarn as I first spin it. With the Navajo technique, one must follow the various stages, or the quality of the yarn will suffer. Too much drafting at the beginning will weaken the spinner as well as the yarn. The over spinning makes it very difficult to pull the yarn out into a smaller strand, and many fibers may be broken from pulling too hard.

Splicing on a new rolag.

Putting in the first light twist.

Applying the second twist.

Pulling out the yarn after applying the second twist.

Pulling out the yarn while applying the third twist.

Applying the final twist.

The wool used by the Navajo has a short-to-medium length staple; it has a medium crimp, but is a coarse and strong fiber with a rough handle. This wool works well with their technique to produce a very dense and durable product. There are easier and faster ways to spin wool, but given the wool that they have to work with and the desire to make strong, durable rugs, the Navajo have developed a method of spinning that may very well produce the best quality possible. Spinning wheels were given to some of the Navajo spinners several years ago; they were tried and rejected. On the wheels, the Navajo were not able to produce the type and quality of yarn that they desired.

When Susie had finished with her demonstrations, the time came for us to leave. Except for me—I wanted to do some spinning. With a lot of gesturing, I was able to indicate that I would like a try at it. Susie thought this was funny, but I picked up the cards, carded up a rolag, and started to spin. I had never used a Navajo spindle; however, I did know the basic idea and I had been watching her very closely.

The first problem was how to sit on the floor comfortably and be able to spin. The legs are tucked under in such a way so as not to interfere with the rolling of the spindle. Susie sat on her feet and ankles. (A month or more of yoga might have been good preparation; a pillow would have helped.) I ended up with one leg straight out, the other tucked under. I also had trouble controlling the spindle. It lies free against your thigh—you just lay your fingertips against the shaft and roll it along your thigh until it gets to the heel of your hand. This is easy enough to do once, but getting it back in place for the second, third, and subsequent rolls takes a lot of skill to do easily and well.

Susie was able to really make the spindle fly. It appeared that at the end of each roll her fingers would cup the spindle shaft and bring it back while it was still spinning around. She would roll it fast, cup it with her fingertips, and have it back in place for the next roll before it would stop spinning. At first it looked as though she rolled only the spindle, and that it was magically always in the right place. For me, it was hard to keep the spindle from continuing to roll forward and off my leg, much to the enjoyment of everyone present.

Ed. Note: Again, rolling the spindle up the thigh to produce a Z-twist has been extensively documented in both ethnographic and weaving circles. On occasion, rolling toward the body has been granted mystic significance by various writers. Yet, by my own observation, I have noted that many, if not most, of the elderly Navajo spinner-weavers spin their singles counterclockwise—rolling the spindle down the thigh to produce S-twist, as described by the author and verified in the photographs. The women spinning in this manner usually live the traditional Navajo lifestyle wearing their turquoise jewelry and velvet-tiered skirts daily, not just for celebrations. As one grandmother pointed out, the skirts interfered with rolling the spindle up the thigh—furthermore, the skirt got "messed up" and in time began to show abrasion from the spindle if spinning Z-twist. P.G-R*

The drafting of the yarn was not difficult to do, but following the various stages was difficult to remember to do. Out of habit, I would draft out into too small of a yarn. Then when I didn't draft out too small, I would not underspin enough so as to be able to pull the yarn into a smaller strand. During this time Susie was not able to help me other than by demonstrating or indicating when it was not being done right.

Some of my yarn was drafted and spun only once, and some of it was done four or five times. Getting the right amount of twist each step of the way is what makes the spinning go well and the yarn come out right. After a while, I was able to do it somewhat the way that Susie wanted me to. My yarn looked all right, but it was probably not as hard and tough as is desirable for Navajo rugs. Susie was very excited and pleased with what I had done, and she indicated that she intended to use it in the rug she was making.

During this visit there was a lot of photographing going on. This is standard procedure, and Susie dressed and acted the part very well. She gave a good demonstration, but with a lot of posturing for the cameras. I keep thinking how it would be to visit her with other spinners *and* no cameras. I suspect that she would like that as well.

At the time of this article, Ron Chacey was the owner and operator of Windsor Farms in southeast Ohio, and was a breeder of natural colored Lincoln and Lincoln crossbred sheep, specifically developed for handspinning wool.

Winter 1983

Chapter Six

SIMPLE HANDSPUN PROJECTS

The following knitted projects are very simple and don't require very much handspun yarn. Although these yarns weren't all spun with a handspindle, your handspindle yarns will certainly work for these projects. They're great for beginners, so take your ball of handspun, pick up your needles, and go for it!

Rule of Thumb:

NBK* Rolled Brim Hat

Betsy Neal

Here's a hat that can be made easily by anyone using anybody's handspun yarn.

First: Knit a 4-inch (10-cm) sample on desired size needles (whatever is handy or comfortable). I like to use a set of short-circular and double-pointed needles that are unoccupied at the moment.

Second: Measure head (or make your best guess) and subtract 2 inches (5 cm). Multiply this number by your gauge and add or subtract a few stitches to end up with a multiple of 8. [1] Using circular or double-pointed needles, loosely cast on this number of stitches. Now label and store your sample in an attempt to get organized.

Join without twisting, placing a marker to show the beginning of each round, and begin to knit. Work around and around in stockinette stitch until it's time to begin the decreases for the crown. There are two ways to tell when to begin decreasing: measuring against your hand, or using a tape measure. Because the hat is worked entirely in stockinette, the bottom edge will roll into a brim. Measure from the rolled edge, not the cast-on edge.

For the "rule of thumb" method, place the palm of your hand at the bottom of the hat on the rolled brim. Using your fingers as a measuring device, start the decreases at: thumb's length for a baby hat (about 4¼"/11 cm); pinkie's length for a child's hat (about 5¼"/13.5 cm); pointer's length for a teen's hat (6¼"/16 cm); ringman's length for a woman's hat (6½"/16.5 cm); and tallman's length for a man's hat (7"/18 cm).

When you begin the decreases, switch to double-pointed needles, if you're not already on them. Shape the top as follows. Row 1: K6, k2tog; repeat around. Rows 2, 4, 6, 8, 10, 12: Knit around. Row 3: K5, k2tog; repeat around. Row 5: K4, k2tog; repeat around. Row 7: K3, k2tog; repeat around. Row 9: K2, k2tog; repeat around. Row 11: K1, k2tog; repeat around. The last row (Row 13) is k2tog, repeat around.[2] Break off yarn and pull through the remaining sts. Fasten off securely inside the hat.

Wash in warm, sudsy water, rinse in cool water, roll in a towel to remove excess moisture, and lay flat to dry, turning occasionally.

Betsy Neal took up spinning and weaving when her daughter added sheep to her 4-H goat project. That daughter is now a 1998 graduate from vet school and Betsy has her own flock of sheep and two dairy goats. Betsy makes time nearly every day to spin, weave, or knit—in addition to teaching second grade in Schenectady, New York.

Summer 1998

*NBK = No Brain Knitting, suitable for car trips, meetings, or sporting events.

[1]*For a testing sample, we used a Lopi-style yarn which worked up at 4 stitches/inch (2.5 cm) on size 8 (5–5.5 mm) needles. The head measurement of the closest person was 21" (53 cm); minus 2" (5 cm) gives 19" (48 cm). Multiplied by the gauge, 19 × 4 = 76 stitches; for a number divisible by 8, we rounded up to 80. Our finished hat used the entire 3.5-ounce (100-g) skein, with no leftovers.*

Very Simple Socks

Kris Paige and Marie Kirk

The easiest sock of all is a simple tube, closed at one end to make a toe. Tube socks don't have any heel shaping—you just pull them on any way, and they'll stretch around your feet. For maximum stretchiness, simple tube socks are knitted in ribbing from cuff to toe.

Spiral rib socks are a popular variation. To make these, you move the ribbing one stitch to the left (or right) every inch or so. For example, on a multiple of 4 stitches, you might k2, p2 around for six rows. Then p1—to move the ribbing one stitch to the left—and resume k2, p2 for another six rows. Again, p1 to move the ribbing and continue like this until the sock is long enough.

At the toe end of any tube sock, straight or spiral rib, you can divide the stitches in half and make standard paired decreases spaced evenly around the sock. This fits comfortably around your toes, but gives the sock an orientation—you have to wear it with the decreases at the sides.

Another approach is to make a round toe that you can roll around and wear in any position. To make a round toe, you knit a series of rows with decreases spaced evenly around the sock. For example, starting with 40 stitches:

First decrease round: *K3, K 2 rounds.
Second decrease round: *K2, k2 tog*.
  K 2 rounds.
Third decrease round: *K1, k2 tog*.
  K2 rounds.
Last decrease round: *K2 tog*.
Draw yarn tail through loops and pull
  tight.

Materials: 4 to 8 ounces (112 - 224 grams) of worsted-weight yarn, and size 8 (5 - 5.5 mm) double-pointed needles (or size to guage).

Gauge: Measured over k1, p1 rib, 3½ sts = 1 inch (2.5 cm), 5 rows = 1 inch (2.5 cm).

Size guidelines: 2 - 4 years: Cast on 24 sts; make sock 8 - 10 inches (20 - 25 cm) long. 4 - 8 years; Cast on 30 sts; make sock 12 - 14 inches (30.5 - 35.5 cm) long. 10 - 12 years: Cast on 36 sts; make sock 16 - 18 inches (40.5 - 45.75 cm) long. Adult: Cast on 40 sts; make sock 18 - 24 inches (45.75 - 61 cm) long.

Following the size and length guidelines listed above, cast on the basic number of stitches and divide on three needles. Work in k1, p1 rib until sock is ½ inch (1.25 cm) shorter than desired length.

Decrease for toe as follows. Divide stitches in half by placing markers on needles. Round 1: *K1, sl 1, k1, psso, k to last 3 sts before marker, k2 tog, k1*, repeat. Round 2: Knit.

Repeat rounds 1 and 2 until 8 (8, 12, 12) sts remain. Graft toe sts together.

Kris Paige and Mare Kirk enjoyed working collaboratively on this project. We hope they'll do more.

Winter 1992

Family Mittens
Lucy Rogers

These patterns were developed especially for speedy knitting on large needles. The body of the mittens uses a double strand of yarn and #10 needles, so the mittens are thick and durable for Maine winters and easy enough for beginning knitters.

The yarn is a singles about the same size as a commercial knitting worsted, spun from natural colors of imported Romney carded together. Each pair requires a hundred yards of yarn.

For the beginning knitter.

Size: 2- to 4-year-old child, and adult small (medium, large).

Yarn: 800 yd/lb (1600 m/kg), 12 wraps/in (19/4 cm). Lucy used a soft handspun single-ply wool similar to Lopi, but less regular in diameter. She carded together natural grays and white for a tweedy effect. The child's mittens require 2 oz (56 g), and the adult sizes require about 4 oz (113 g).

Gauge: With larger needles over stockinette at 7 sts = 2 in (11 st = 8 cm).

Child's Mitten Instructions: With smaller needles cast on 24 sts. Work k 1, p 1 rib for 18 rnds. Change to st st and larger needles and add another strand of yarn from the other end of the ball (wind ball so that yarn is available from both ends). Knit 7 rnds plain.

Thumb gusset: A beg of next rnd, inc 1 st in first st, k 3, inc 1 st in next st, k to end of rnd—26 sts. Knit 2 more rnds. S1 first 7 sts of rnd to holder for thumb. Join rem sts for hand—19 sts. Knit 12 rnds plain, then begin finger tip shaping.

Finger tip shaping: (K 2 tog, k 2) 4 times, k 3—15 sts. Knit 1 rnd plain.

Next rnd: (K 1, k2 tog) around—10 sts.

Following rnd: K2 tog around—5 sts. K 2 tog once (this is a partial rnd)—4 sts. Fasten off.

Thumb: Divide 7 thumb sts on 3 needles; pick up 2 sts on inside of thumb—9 sts. Work 1 rnd. Next rnd: Dec 1 st by knitting 2 tog—8 sts. Knit 8 rnds.

Thumb: Divide 7 thumb sts on 3 needles; pick up 2 sts on inside of thumb—9 sts. Work 1 rnd. Next rnd: Dec 1 st by knitting 2 tog—8 sts. Knit 8 rnds.

Dec for thumb: K 2 tog around—4 sts. Fasten off. Make second mitten the same.

Adult Mitten Instructions: With smaller needles cast on 32 (34, 36) sts. Divide on 3 needles. Work in k 1, p 1 rib for 4 in (10 cm).

Thumb gusset: Rnd 1: Change to st st and knit next rnd, dec 6 sts evenly spaced around—26 (28, 30) sts. Change to larger needles and add a second strand of yarn (wind ball so yarn is available from both ends).

Rnd 2: Inc 1 st in first st, k 1, inc 1 st in next st, k to end of rnd—28 (30, 32) sts.

Rnds 3 and 4: Knit.

Rnd 5: Inc 1 st in first st, k 3, inc 1 st in next st, k to end of rnd—30 (32, 34) sts.

Rnds 6 and 7: Knit.

Rnd 8: Inc 1 st first st, k 5, inc 1 st in next st, k to end of rnd—32 (34, 36) sts

Rnds 9 and 10: Knit

Rnd 11: Inc 1 st in first st, k 7, inc 1 st in next st, k to end of rnd—34 (36, 38) sts

Rnds 12 and 13: Knit

Thumb opening: S1 first 11 sts of rnd to holder for thumb. Cast on 1 st and join for hand—24 (26, 28) sts. Knit to within 1" (2½ cm) of desired length.

Finger tip shaping: Rnd 1: (K 2, k2 tog) around (size medium only, end k 2)—18 (20, 21) sts.

Rnd 2: Knit.

Rnd 3: (K 1, k 2 tog) around (size medium only, end k 2)—12 (14, 14) sts.

Rnd 4: K 2 tog around—6 (7, 7) sts.

Rnd 5: K 2 tog two (three, three) times (this is a partial rnd)—4 sts. Fasten off.

Thumb: Divide 11 thumb sts from holder on 3 needles. Pick up 2 sts on inside of thumb—13 sts. Work even 1 rnd. On next rnd dec 1 st on inside of thumb—12 sts. Knit to desired length.

Dec for thumb: Next rnd: K 2 tog around—6 sts

Following rnd: K 2 tog twice (this is a partial rnd) 4—sts.

Fasten off. Make second mitten the same.

Lucy Rogers lives in Lovell, Maine. She owns Hilltop Handspun and hopes people's hands will stay warm with her easy, quick pattern.

Homespun, Handknit,
Interweave Press, 1987

Knitted Merino Scarf

Erda Kappeler

A friend returning from Australia brought me some heavenly Merino roving. I spun it into a two-ply yarn of about sportweight, and designed the pattern for this scarf. Inspired by work I had seen in a Burda publication called Grosses Strickmusterkeft (big knit sample magazine), my concept consists of columns of lace arches separated by columns of a lacy rib.

This is an ideal travel project—one ball of yarn, lightweight bamboo needles, a pattern that repeats in a few rows, and no shaping.

Size: The finished scarf measures about 60 inches (152 cm) long by 8 inches (20 cm) wide.

Yarn: Spun at 3,500 yards per pound (7,056 m/kg) and 20 wraps per inch (2.5 cm): 1¾ ounces (50 g).

Gauge: 6 stitches = 1 inch (2.5 cm) measured over stockinette stitch.

Needles: Pair of straight needles, size 7 (4.5 mm), or size needed to achieve gauge.

Cast on 53 sts and work 5 rows garter stitch (the first row is a reverse-side row). Begin pattern as follows:

Row 1: K3, * ssk, yo, k1, yo, k2tog, k1, yo, k2, sl1, k2tog, psso, k2, yo, k1*; rep from * to * twice, ssk, yo, k1, yo, k2tog, k3.

Rows 2, 4, and 6: K3, p47, k3.

Row 3: K3, * ssk, yo, k1, yo, k2tog, k2, yo, k1, sl1, k2tog, psso, k1, yo, k2*; rep from * to * twice, ssk, yo, k1, yo, k2tog, k3.

Row 5: K3, * ssk, yo, k1, yo, k2tog, k3, yo, sl1, k2tog, psso, yo, k3*; rep from * to * twice, ssk, yo, k1, yo, k2tog, k3.

Repeat rows 1 to 6 until the scarf measures about 59½ inches (151 cm) long or the length you prefer. Work 5 rows garter stitch and bind off loosely.

Erda Kappeler, of Ukiah, California, learned to use a spindle in 1963. A year later, her mother-in-law gave her the wheel she still spins on.

Winter 1999

☐	k on face, p on reverse
⊡	p on face, k on reverse
◣	ssk
◢	k2tog
⋊	sl 1, k2tog, psso
⊙	yo

repeat 3 times

A Very Simple Vest

Ruth Barbour

Here's a simple pattern, suitable for hand knitting in a hurry with bulky-weight yarn.

Sizes: See schematic for specific measurements, chest measurement of finished sweater is twice the width measurement at the bottom—in order, 38" (96 cm), 40" (102 cm), 42" (107 cm), 44" (112 cm). Instructions are written for 38" finished chest, with other sizes in parentheses.

Needles: Size 10 (6-6.5 mm) needles, or size needed to obtain correct gauge for body; size 8 (5 - 5.5 mm) needles for ribbing (or two sizes smaller than body size).

Pattern: Rows 1 - 10: Stockinette st (knit across on right side [odd] rows, purl across on wrong side rows), 11 - 14: Garter st (knit across on all rows). Repeat sequence of 14 rows.

Body: Make two identical pieces, as follows. Using smaller needles, cast on 49 (53, 57, 61) sts. Knit k 2, p 2 ribbing for 10 rows.

Change to larger needles and knit 36 (38, 40, 42) rows, maintaining pattern. Mark underarm on each side.

Continue to knit for 28 (32, 34, 34) more rows, maintaining pattern.

Bind off 16 sts, and place a marker for edge of neckline. Bind off next 17 (21, 25, 29) sts, and

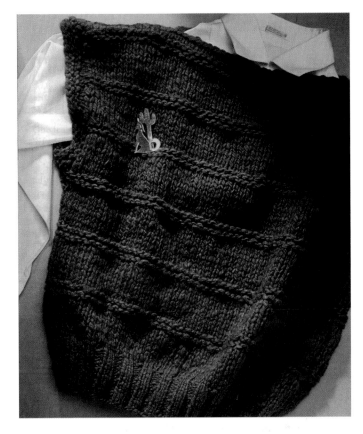

place another marker for opposite edge of neckline. Bind off remaining 16 sts.

Armhole: Pick up 22 (23, 25, 25) sts between armhole marker and top outside edge of shoulder, with right side of fabric facing you. P 1 row, k 1 row; bind off. Do this on both sides of the body piece.

Finishing: Sew shoulder and side seams. Steam block, keeping pressure very light to prevent distortion of garter-st rows.

Ruth Barbour lives in Bahama, North Carolina. The yarn for this sweater was dyed with Lanaset. Her first fiber was a generic "combed American top."

Summer 1984

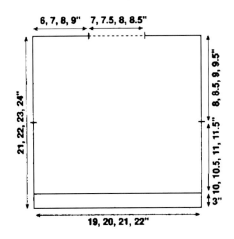

Vest Plan:

6, 7, 8, 9"   7, 7.5, 8, 8.5"

21, 22, 23, 24"

8, 8.5, 9, 9.5"

8.5, 9, 11, 11.5"

10, 10.5, 11, 11.5"

3"

19, 20, 21, 22"

Index

Numbers in *italics* indicate illustrations; numbers in **bold face** indicate photographs.

Pure spinning
SATISFACTION

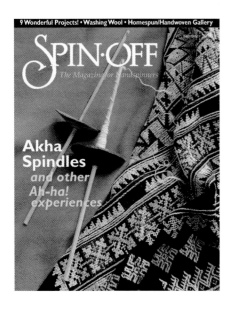

Show-and-tell with the world's most creative spinners will inspire you. Solid, accurate technical information, plus tips and tricks from lifetimes of spinning will add new facets to your spinning know-how. Our coverage and celebration of the spinning community will connect you with other spinners who share your passion. Spin with *Spin·Off*, your hands will say ahhh and your brain will say ah-ha!. How can you spin without it?

Spin·Off $24 (4 issues)
P.O. Box 495 • Mount Morris, IL 61054-0495 • 800-767-9638

Find these books at your favorite craft source

Handspun Treasures from Rare Wools
Collected Works from the Save the Sheep Project

Edited by Deborah Robson

Bringing together the art of spinning and wools from rare breeds of sheep, *Handspun Treasures from Rare Wools* catalogs the 29 touring pieces from the Save the Sheep project. Complete with basic spinning terms and concepts.

8½ × 9, paperbound, 96 pages, color photos.
#1035—$19.95

Tops with a Twist
A Special Publication from Spin·Off *Magazine*

Hats are what you'll find in this special publication developed from the collection of fabulous, inventive entries submitted to *Spin·Off*'s hat contest. There are 17 fun and funky hats to knit and 1 to crochet with close-up photographs, accompanied by easy-to-understand instructions.

8½ × 9, paperbound, 80 pages, illustrations and color photos.
#1026—$14.95

The Gossamer Webs Design Collection
Three Orenburg Shawls to Knit

Design Interpretation by Galina Khmeleva

Unique knitted lace masterpieces from the Orenburg region of Russia, Galina Khmeleva has diligently worked to chart and preserve the indigenous textile art form of Gossamer style lace shawls. Create your own heirloom shawl following charts and step-by-step instructions.

8½ × 11, paperbound, 56 pages, photos and charts.
#1091—$12.95

or call 800-272-2193

or visit our website at www.interweave.com